ENDORSEM

CW01020775

A readable, well researched, well-reasoned book, ~~~~ ~~~~~ support of women throughout the Bible. Comprehensive, logical, and clear, this book is an indispensable treatment of women in the Bible. I enthusiastically recommend it to anyone eager to hear God's high regard for women or anyone who wrestles with the Bible's teaching on women.

> Rev. Dr. Grace Y. May, Associate Professor of Biblical Studies and Director of the Women's Institute, William Carey International University

I have read most of the books written by complementarians and evangelical egalitarians and I think Philip Payne's are the best. It is the fruit of forty years of study by a first-rate biblical scholar who does not avoid any difficult issues. The scholarly depth and the clarity of his writing is exceptional.

> Kevin Giles, Anglican pastor and theologian

A compelling and highly readable case for the full equality of women and men. This remarkable book presents the best in New Testament scholarship for non-specialists.

> Harold Netland
> Professor of Philosophy of Religion and Intercultural Studies
> Trinity Evangelical Divinity School

If you need a book that quickly and clearly exposes the failed teachings of male-headship arguments, this is it! Respected by Christians the world over, Phil Payne's research opens new doors of leadership for women.

> Mimi Haddad Ph.D., President of CBE International

If any reader wants to understand the egalitarian view of subjects such as head covering or a woman's submission to her husband, this is the book to read. This is an easy-to-read and must-have book for any serious reader on the equality of man and woman in Christ.

> KeumJu Jewel Hyun, Founder and President, Matthew 28 Ministries, Inc. and Adjunct Professor of Theology of Work, Bakke Graduate University, Dallas, Texas.

I highly value Philip for both his integrity and profound scholarship. *Why Can't Women Do That?* is readable and easily understood. I give this book my highest recommendation.

      Dr. Felicity Dale: author, *The Black Swan Effect*

Philip Payne's work has been among the most recommended resources for explaining and defending evangelical gender egalitarianism. This new volume is written for a broad readership.

      Jeff Miller, editor of *Priscilla Papers*

I heartily recommend this new book. You will be challenged by its careful exegesis and thoughtful exposition.

      Randy Colver, Fairburn, GA

This is a great gift. Its popular rhetoric contributes to clarity and makes the argument even more persuasive. Payne's disciplined study brings us ever so close to the original texts of scripture.

      Richard F. Kantzer, Holland Michigan

Philip Payne's work on this subject has been an invaluable resource to me. His own authentic journey on the topic makes him an excellent guide. I am deeply grateful for his scholarship!

      Dr. R. Scott Lisea
      Campus Pastor at Westmont College

You are welcome to email Philip B. Payne directly at **philip.b.payne@ gmail.com** or Vince Huffaker at v**ince@vinatipress.com** with corrections, questions, and other feedback regarding this book. Please identify how you want your name and institution or state to be cited in any endorsement.

Emailing **philip.b.payne@gmail.com** constitutes your permission for Phil to quote from your message (without your contact information) on the **www.pbpayne.com** website.

You are welcome to see Philip B. Payne's interaction with questions raised about this book, supplemental information about the book, including the complete, up-to-date bibliography, and free downloads of articles by P. B. Payne at **www.pbpayne.com**.

WHY CAN'T
WOMEN
Do That?

Breaking Down the Reasons
Churches Put Men in Charge

PHILIP B. PAYNE *and* VINCE HUFFAKER

VINATI
—PRESS—

Published by Vinati Press, Boulder, CO, 80303. **www.vinatipress.com**

Library of Congress Control Number: 2021922114

Trade Paperback ISBN: 979-8-9851174-0-0
Hardcover ISBN: 979-8-9851174-2-4
eBook ISBN: 979-8-9851174-1-7

The Greek, Hebrew, and transliteration fonts used in this book are available from **www.linguistsoftware.com**.

2022-02-14

*This book is dedicated to
Adena, Rick, and Barbara
for forming its vision and voice,
and giving it wings.*

CONTENTS

Foreword and Acknowledgements

Dear reader,

You hold in your hand a labor of love that has taken over ten years to complete. I (Vince) ask your indulgence as I reminisce a bit.

Phil and I met over ten years ago and discovered we were each writing the same book, but from two different directions.

Phil's trajectory is perhaps the more familiar. At the time, Phil had recently written a theological masterpiece, *Man and Woman: One in Christ.* It is a phenomenal book and a thorough treatise on the subject of male-female equality, but it was very hard to read for lay persons like me. Many people had been asking Phil for an easier-to-read version of that book, and he had begun working on his version of this book, trying to figure out what that would look like.

When I read books on the subject, including Phil's book, I realized there were satisfying explanations of all the controversial verses that people typically raise against women in leadership. However, while there were many relevant books, I couldn't find the "goldilocks" book with just the right balance of breadth and depth for a wide audience. Since I couldn't find the book I wanted, I decided to start writing it myself.

I knew that simply laying out the theology would not be sufficient. Even if I proved the Bible says women can be church leaders, that wouldn't change anything if people believed men were just better leaders, or if they didn't want to abandon a church "tradition" of male-only leadership, or if they were scared of a "slippery slope" of female leadership. My book would have to address both the theological issues and many of those common concerns.

I wanted to bring in somebody to help write the opening, non-theological part of the book, so I asked around and was introduced to Tim Krueger. Tim came on board and helped find the voice and tone of the book, and I am thankful for his help.

Then I met Phil and we realized our skills were complementary, so we decided to join forces. Although I enjoy writing when time permits and have a passion for this topic, my experience is mainly in software development, which entails breaking down large complex requirements into code that is as simple as it can be (and no simpler). It took ten years to take over five hundred pages of Phil's theological descriptions and shrink them into about 120 pages and make the logical flow as simple as it can be (and no simpler).

All along the way, I have been accompanied and supported by my wonderful wife and star editor, Julie Huffaker. She read through countless edits, constantly finding issues, and pressing me on with phrases such as:

- "This doesn't make sense."
- "What are you trying to say here?"
- "Well, it doesn't say that."
- "You keep using that word; I do not think it means what you think it means." (We are *Princess Bride* fans.)

Additionally, I'd like to give big thanks to Mimi Haddad. She and the crew at Christians for Biblical Equality (CBE) International (**cbeinternational.org**) run an amazing organization that is at the forefront of restoring God's plan for equal partnership between men and women. It was Mimi who introduced me to both Tim and Phil (Tim was working at CBE at the time).

If you desire to send us any feedback regarding this book, I invite you to send it to me at **vince@vinatipress.com** and/or to Phil at **philip.b.payne@gmail.com**.

Thank you!

Vince Huffaker
Vinati Press

Prologue

Dear Uncle Johnny,

It was great to see you and Aunt Grace this summer. Thank you for your wonderful hospitality, as always. It was fun catching up with you and getting a tour of the city. And I was intrigued by your church. It was, shall we say, different from what I expected.

Which brings me to the point of this letter. I will just spit it out. Your church confused me! Women were up front leading during the church service. And as I read more about the church, I realized your church has women deacons and elders. But I thought you believed that only men could lead the church and the family. So, what happened? When did you change? And why? I am just not sure where this new liberal side of you is coming from. Don't you have to ignore a lot of the Bible, including some important teachings, to come to such conclusions?

Maybe it sounds old-fashioned, but I believe that men have a special God-given sense of responsibility and leadership. I know the Bible plainly teaches that men should be the leaders of the church and in the family, and this is what Christians have believed for almost two thousand years. If we throw that out, then what else will we throw out? I am sure you have noticed the devastating effects of all the sexual sins that our society now deems normal—sins that arise from not respecting the differences between men and women. And besides, men are just naturally better leaders. Why would we not simply keep developing and encouraging male leaders? Are there really so few men available to fill the leadership roles? Are we going to deny good male leaders a chance at leadership in order to let women in?

And what about families? If no one is the clear leader of a family, then how are the tough decisions supposed to be made? Women are certainly equal in value to men, but men have the God-designed role to lead. What you are saying just sounds like feminism, putting women into a place of power over men. Are my wife and I supposed to trade responsibilities now? Should I stay home and cook, while Ruth works on a construction job or something? Am I supposed to give up watching football, or should Ruth give up her sewing business? No. God's way is simple, pure, and beautiful. Men are masculine, and women are feminine. Uncle Johnny, I am afraid you have been duped, and I am concerned about you.

Okay, I have said enough. Please forgive me for being so blunt. Our pastor recently led a sermon series on this topic, so it is still very fresh in my mind. I hope you will humor my challenge, and I look forward to your response.

Love, your nephew,
Theo

P.S. Ruth sends her love.

Dear Theo,

Thank you for your letter! I am honored that you feel free to share your concerns with me and that you welcome my response. We enjoyed your visit with us so much, and we can hardly wait for you to come back again.

I guess I should start by confessing. As you suspect, I do believe that men and women are equal when it comes to issues of leadership, gifts, authority, etc. And, yes, as you properly recall, I used to believe the opposite. In fact, some years ago I heard a lecturer state that nothing in Scripture limits the ministry of women. I was so sure he was wrong that I almost shouted, "That's not true!" In fact, I was so determined to prove he was wrong that I started studying the Greek passages so I could detail all the lecturer's mistakes. But the more I dug into it, the more I discovered that I was the one who was wrong.

I appreciate you expressing your concern, and I'll do my best to respond to it. "Women in leadership" is a very big topic, however, so it will require a much bigger letter to go through it. I have been meaning to write up my beliefs about this very topic as simply and clearly as possible, so I'll gladly take advantage of your letter and use it as an excuse to do so.

Before I do, however, let me reassure you that we both still worship the same God. The basics of my faith have not wavered at all. I still hold fast to the fantastic and incredible truths that the one true God sent his Son, Jesus, to die on the cross for our sins to restore us to himself; Jesus rose from the dead on the third day; he is the one and only way to heaven; and God's Holy Spirit is actively at work in all believers even today. I still believe that the Bible is God's Word to us, inerrant as it was originally inspired and written, and that we should strive to follow its teachings.

And believe me, I understand what you are saying. As I read the Bible, I realize that it is full of examples of men who were in charge (and many fewer examples of women in charge). The first human was a man. Israel's official priests were men. Almost all the authors of the Bible were men. Jesus was a man and chose twelve male apostles. The Bible calls wives to submit to their husbands. God is referred to as Father. The list goes on and on.

In general, the Bible seems to focus primarily on men from Genesis to Revelation, and very little in it indicates that God objects to this state of affairs. So, I completely understand your skepticism. It might even sound like the debate is over and there is nothing left to discuss. Remember, however, that just like the Bible's description of polygamous marriages or slavery should not be interpreted as their endorsement, the Bible's description of almost exclusively male leadership should not be interpreted as an endorsement of almost exclusively male leadership.

When we look closer, there is a much stronger undercurrent throughout the Bible:

- An undercurrent of the Holy Spirit filling the church with believers who are gifted in special and unique ways to expand God's kingdom.
- An undercurrent of the oneness of the body of Christ (the church) and the priesthood of all believers (women too).
- An undercurrent of humility, service, and mutual submission among all Christians.
- An undercurrent of the freedom that Christ gives and the all-important total focus on the preeminence of Christ and spreading the gospel.

It is this undercurrent that I claim is the better way. I believe this is actually the Bible's focus.

Finally, you ask why this topic even matters. Here are two reasons. First, the church is supposed to advance God's kingdom. But when the leadership and teaching gifts of women are ignored, or even limited, this undermines the advancement of God's kingdom. These gifts should be used in the most productive ways possible to advance God's kingdom, without regard to the gender of the person who has the gifts. Second, the church is supposed to be the purveyor of truth. When it pursues something that is not the truth, the church's credibility is tarnished.

Looking around us, I do not think we can honestly say that women are not suited for leadership. After all, women are currently successfully filling every possible role in society (including scientists, engineers, politicians, teachers, and CEOs of gigantic international corporations). Surely you can sense that something is not quite right with the idea that women are not allowed to teach biblical truths to men (only to children or other women), or to oversee a church congregation, or that they must defer to their husbands in all decisions? I am not suggesting that just because it does not feel right, this means it cannot be right, only that maybe it warrants a second look.

I would love to talk with you more about this, and I welcome the chance to write down more complete responses to all the issues you raised and to address all the relevant Bible passages. Please give me some time, and I will send you my completed letter. I warn you—it will be a long letter. And I fully understand that words on a page do not change hearts—only the Holy Spirit can do that. I pray that we will both have discernment as we talk further about the issue.

Give a hug to Ruth from me!

Love,
Uncle Johnny

Introduction

⌒

Dear Theo,

Okay, I finished my write-up, and here it is! Sorry it took me so long. I will start by going through the various concerns you raised, like discussing the idea that men are just naturally better leaders. Afterward, I will go through every Bible passage I could find that deals with the topic of male and female leadership.

I know it is a lot to go over in one fell swoop, but I look forward to hearing what you think about it.

Love,
Uncle Johnny

Part One

LEADERSHIP CONCERNS AND CHURCH TRADITION

Identity in Christ

Theo, you mentioned that men should be masculine and women should be feminine. I would never suggest that you stop watching football, college or pro, nor would I say you need to start cooking. I am in no way suggesting that you should stop loving sports, being a leader, hunting, or doing any other so-called manly things that do not violate God's commandments. I know that several Christian leaders suggest there is a crisis of masculinity, of men not taking responsibility for themselves and their families. Instead, they are living in a sort of extended boyhood. The solution, they say, is to step up to the plate, find a job, get married, have a family, and lead and support that family. Then, men will be living within God's design for their lives, making their families more functional and becoming more fulfilled. Some say that if a man does not step up, not only is he sinning by neglecting his God-given responsibilities, he is also forcing his wife to sin by stepping out of her designated role. She is forced to take over his roles, neglecting her own.

I am not saying that men or women should neglect God's design for their lives. I do not advocate "effeminate" men or "masculine" women. I am not suggesting that a man cannot be the sole breadwinner or that there is something wrong with a woman who chooses to be a stay-at-home mom. If a man drives a pickup, bench presses 250 pounds, watches football (though some might argue rugby is a more manly sport), and does whatever other manly things he loves to do, good for him. If a woman loves getting her nails done, cooking for her husband, and reading romance novels, good for her. If this is what God has called these two people to, then they ought to do those things with heart, mind, and soul.

I am not contending that men and women ought never to behave in these ways. What I do suggest is that God did not design all men to love all the activities I mentioned or to participate in them, nor did God design all women to think and behave in the same way. Men and women both find their identity ultimately in Christ, not in the activities they do or the jobs they have. The Bible teaches that the gospel of Christ frees both men and women by grounding them in a new identity in Christ. It calls for mutual leadership, love, respect, and submission in the marriage relationship and in the church. If God calls a woman to preach, then she should preach. If God calls a man to be a stay-at-home dad, he should be one. If they are gifted in ways that fall into traditional roles, they should use those gifts as God leads.

A biblical view of manhood and womanhood is one that encourages all people, regardless of gender, to develop their God-given gifts to their fullest potential. Whether in marriage or in the church, these individual gifts complement each other to build a unity that reflects the love and unity of the Trinity.

And in a marriage, both spouses should use their unique gifts equally to lead and direct their family. Neither spouse should have exclusive authority to make the final decision. Think about your friendships. Does one friend always decide what to do or where to go? Of course not, but are your relationships crippled? I doubt it! The Bible does not teach that the husband always has the "final word." Rather, the posture of all believers should be the posture of a servant. To insist that in the real world, someone needs to be able to put their foot down, is contrary to what Christ came to earth to do. This may work in armies, in business, and in politics, but it undermines Christian relationships. On the contrary, if two Christians mutually love and respect one another and together seek God's guidance, God will guide them to mutual agreement, even if it may not be ideal for either person. The question should not be, "Who has the final word, men or women?" This assumes that one of them must have it. Only God has the final word, and he has the power to guide his people to a place where they can mutually agree to move ahead.

Christian community and Christian family, as taught in the Bible, require that we as humans share jointly in family decision-making, shepherding in a church, teaching, protecting, helping, and supporting. Any crises of masculinity and femininity in today's world are due to a failure to adhere to God's biblical design, not to crossing traditional role boundaries. We have no right to limit the use of God's gifts to roles assigned by culture instead of by the guidance of the Holy Spirit consistent with the gospel of Christ.

To tie these ideas together with actual practice, consider the Seattle Seahawks of the NFL. No, seriously, hear me out. Pete Carroll, coach of the Seahawks, gave excellent insights about his relationship with the general manager, John Schneider:

> We work our way to the point where we agree on everything, and that's through give and take and really great conversation and respect for one another. In any relationship, you've got to serve the relationship. You've got to give everything you can to it to make it the most it can possibly be, and that's what we've done. It's putting the other person first and trying to work tirelessly to understand them, to serve them, to help them be the best they can be in hopes that they will do the same so that you can expedite and facilitate the whole relationship. And it's all based on respect—the regard that you hold the other person in and then how you act and treat them.[1]

I believe that all Christians, especially husbands and wives, should treat each other the way Pete Carroll describes his relationship with John Schneider.

---

1. http://www.espn.com/blog/seattle-seahawks/post/_/id/18960/why-the-pete-carroll-john-schneider-relationship-has-served-the-seahawks-well.

Keeping it "Simple"

In your letter, Theo, you spoke about everything being "simple" if we stick to the idea that men should be masculine and women should be feminine. What does that mean, exactly? How does the Bible define masculinity or femininity? Many books and sermons try to explain biblical manhood or biblical womanhood—how to be a better man or woman of God by emphasizing the "proper" traits for your gender. Their authors desire to find and explain a simple, yet deep, spiritual, mystical difference between men and women, a difference beyond the obvious physical differences. Unfortunately, they have never been able to identify a spiritual characteristic that is uniquely manly or womanly. For example, I looked through several of these books and compiled a list. Look at the following characteristics they have described as either "for men" or "for women." Can you tell me which are which?

Courageous	Loyal	Self-Disciplined	Godly
Virtuous	Industrious	Wise	Kind
God-Fearing	Having Integrity	Humble	Honorable

Okay, that was a trick question. Some were identified as manly by one author and womanly by another. Surely you see that these are desirable attributes that all Christians should be pursuing, attributes that any parent would want their daughter or son to pursue. There doesn't seem to be a simple way to differentiate "masculine" and "feminine" characteristics.

But what about leadership? Can't we just say that "men should lead; women should follow"? Even that supposedly simple rule is hard to apply in practice. Extensive research (and universal experience) has proven without a doubt that men and women are equal in overall intelligence, so most churches are not trying to silence women altogether. But that complicates matters. Women are not allowed to teach during church, but they can "share." But that sharing can't be too much like teaching, and she shouldn't stand too close to the pulpit. A woman may write a theological book, but she cannot read it in church. Women cannot read Scripture up front during the church service, but they can sing it. Women cannot teach men, but they can teach boys, if the boys are still children. Women can have authority over men, like a traffic cop directing traffic or an air-traffic controller directing airplanes, but not if the authority is too personally interactive because that might offend a man's sensibilities. The list of ambiguous situations goes on and on with no clear biblical mandate.

On the other hand, my view is simple to understand: men and women working side by side as equals with no restriction based on their gender.

Slippery Slope

Some fear that if we decide women have as much authority and responsibility as men do, then we will fall down a slippery slope to all kinds of sexual sins.

In addition to the issue of equality, other issues related to sex and gender are coming to the forefront. Many people tend to lump all these issues together and assume that if you accept one, you accept them all. But these are all different issues. People who are seeking guidance from the Bible will be led to different sets of verses for each issue. And the verses which inform one issue are typically not relevant for the others. So, there is no slippery slope here for those who are sincerely seeking the Holy Spirit.

Additionally, we need to be careful not to carry the slippery slope argument to an extreme—that argument could be made about literally any decision. Someone might argue that our children should never leave the house because then they will meet other kids who will influence them negatively, leading to drugs, sex, teen pregnancy, and economic irresponsibility, resulting in generations of turmoil. If someone made this argument, we would probably consider them paranoid. Yet, we hear essentially the same argument about the leadership of women. We understand that in real life, every decision opens both positive and negative possibilities, and we have to navigate our lives with wisdom and discernment. The same is true of decisions involving theology and faith. We should not be paralyzed by fear but should live with all our energy guided by God's written word and the Holy Spirit's direction.

If Christians fear all change in their walk with Christ, their growth will be stunted. Many things we currently believe were once controversial but became accepted as believers proceeded with caution, seeking to avoid extremes that could lead them astray. May the Holy Spirit use our concerns to keep us from going astray and guide us to walk the path of obedience to Scripture. We do not know what we might or might not proceed to believe if we adopt any particular view. But Scripture assures us that God will guide those who ask for guidance.

Men are Naturally Better Leaders, Part 1

Kevin O'Leary, also known as "Mr. Wonderful" on ABC's *Shark Tank*, runs a large venture capital fund that is currently vested in about thirty companies, each with annual revenues ranging from five million to 350 million dollars. A few years ago, his auditor suggested they examine the companies to determine which ones were doing well and were deserving of more investment, and which ones were doing poorly and should be written off as a loss. Along the way, they decided to study the successful ones to determine their common attributes. I will let Mr. O'Leary tell you the rest:

> Lo and behold, I had never noticed this, because I wasn't looking. But, not just some of my returns, but 100 percent of my returns came from companies either owned or run by women![2]

As a result, Mr. O'Leary is now studying what makes women such great leaders and is trying to apply those lessons to male leaders. Don't worry, I'm not suggesting that men make bad leaders. Mr. O'Leary may just be better at choosing quality female leaders than quality male leaders. But his findings fit a larger pattern identifying women who are fantastic leaders. For example, currently women are the CEOs of many Fortune 500 companies, including General Motors, Best Buy, Oracle, Northrop Grumman, AutoNation, General Dynamics, and Advanced Micro Devices. Many more women are in all levels of executive positions. Women are also leaders of many countries, including Angela Merkel, chancellor of Germany since 2005, and Erna Solberg, prime minister of Norway since 2013. And, as I write this letter, the vice president of the USA is Kamala Harris.

Are they the exception? Maybe they are among the few women who happen to possess those key leadership qualities that are primarily associated with men. If we believe that men are naturally better leaders, then there must be some masculine quality that is a great attribute for leadership, and unique to men,

---

2. https://www.youtube.com/watch?v=glMU6ZL4UYs.

or at least much more common in men. What could this unique masculine leadership quality be? *Forbes* published a list of eight qualities that make a great leader:

- sincere enthusiasm
- integrity
- great communication skills
- loyalty

- decisiveness
- managerial competence
- empowerment
- charisma[3]

And *Inc.com* published a list of five essential qualities of a great leader:

- clarity
- decisiveness
- courage

- passion
- humility[4]

None of those attributes are exclusive to men. Some of those might even be labeled as stereotypically feminine.

So, after all that, and understanding that many women can and do have all the attributes of a great leader, do you still think men are naturally better leaders? Yes, yes, you probably do. A 2008 Pew Research Center study found just this. It asked people to rank eight traits of good leaders: honest, intelligent, hardworking, decisive, ambitious, compassionate, outgoing, and creative. Then, they asked whether those traits were truer of men or women. On four of the eight traits, women scored higher than men. On three more, they tied. Men were ranked higher on only one trait—decisiveness. Yet, even though the respondents ranked women as equal or higher on seven of the eight most important leadership traits, 20 percent of them still thought men made better leaders (only 6 percent of them said that women make better leaders).[5] Suffice it to say that our internal biases run deep, but they are probably not accurate.

---

3. https://www.forbes.com/sites/kimberlyfries/2018/02/08/8-essential-qualities-that-define-great-leadership.

4. https://www.inc.com/peter-economy/the-5-essential-qualities-of-a-great-leader.html.

5. Paul Taylor, Rich Morin, D'Vera Cohn, April Clark, and Wendy Wang, "A Paradox in Public Attitudes: Men or Women: Who's the Better Leader," Pew Research Center, August 25, 2008, online at https://www.pewresearch.org/social-trends/2008/08/25/men-or-women-whos-the-better-leader/.

Men are Naturally Better Leaders, Part 2

It seems that women can be just as good (or even better) leaders than men, given the right environment. But all too often throughout history, women have been strongly discouraged from pursuing leadership roles (to put it mildly). However, the right environment is crucial for developing and demonstrating skills. People rise or fall according to the expectations put on them.

In a famous landmark study, researchers gave a test to black undergraduate students at Stanford University.[6] On half of the tests, they indicated that it was a test of intelligence, and on the other half of the tests, there was no such indication. The students who thought they were taking an intelligence test scored 50 percent worse than the other students who were taking the exact same test.

After this study came out, a flood of similar research was performed that verified these results for people of various ages, genders, ethnicities, talents, etc. It turns out everybody is susceptible to expectations affecting their performance. For example, another study gathered a bunch of white, religious, math-loving, male, undergraduate college students and gave them a math test. They should have all scored extremely well. However, half of the students were told beforehand that this test was meant to help researchers understand why Asian American students were so much better at math than white students. After the test, those students who thought they were taking a test to compare against their "better" Asian American counterparts scored over 30 percent worse than the other students who took the exact same test.[7]

So, thinking that men are better leaders than women seems a bit unfair, since women have not been permitted to develop their leadership skills for much

6. C. M. Steele & J. Aronson, "Stereotype Threat and the Intellectual Test Performance of African Americans," *Journal of Personality and Social Psychology* 69, no. 5 (1995) 797–811.
7. J. Aronson, M. J. Lustina, C. Good, and K. Keough, "When White Men Can't Do Math: Necessary and Sufficient Factors in Stereotype Threat," *Journal of Experimental Social Psychology* 35 (1999) 29–46.

of history and have been told men are better leaders. It would be like a person who uses a wheelchair suddenly regaining full use of their legs and then being immediately judged on their ability to jump rope.

But even if the environment is supportive, would that be enough? Are there some attributes of intelligence that are clearly associated with being male or female? If so, then simply changing the environment would not be able to change those traits, would it? We often assume that men or women are simply naturally better at one thing or another. However, this is not necessarily true.

When scientists study men and women, they do observe differences. But what is the reason for these differences? Are they natural and based on gender, or are they caused by the way our cultures treat boys and girls and men and women differently? How could we distinguish the effects of fundamental biological differences from the effects of cultural expectations?

One common stereotype is that men are better than women at 3D spatial visualization. To verify this, we would need to test if that difference is a fundamental difference between men and women and thereby impossible to overcome, a cultural difference between men and women that is easily overcome if the culture changes, or a difference that is partly cultural and partly genetic that could gradually change with a change in culture. But we cannot just take a bunch of newborn babies and randomly assign them to different cultures to see how they develop over their lifetime. We would need to find two different cultures, one patriarchal and one matriarchal, that were originally from a single community (so they have much the same genetic makeup) but were separated from each other long enough ago for each culture to have had a chance to adapt to its distinctive beliefs.

Believe it or not, Theo, it turns out that such cultures exist![8] In India, two nearby tribes originally came out of a single tribe, so they are genetically related (so their "nature" is similar), but one tribe became matriarchal and the other patriarchal. Researchers went to these tribes and performed a test to measure

---

8. "Khasi Villagers Display No Sex Differences in Spatial Ability," August 30, 2011, online at http://www.sinlung.com/2011/08/khasi-villagers-display-no-sex.html.

the spatial visualization capability of the men and women in each tribe. In the patriarchal tribe, the women performed significantly worse than the men. In the matriarchal tribe, the women performed just as well as the men.

In summary, it is difficult to prove that either sex is naturally better than the other at a specific task.

Women have historically been restricted from being leaders. But inside an environment that supports and expects women to be strong leaders, we know they can and have become fantastic and successful leaders—just as successful as male leaders.

Breaking with Tradition, Part 1

From the earliest times, Christians have been suspicious of ideas that have appeared to be new. Often rightly so—this suspicion has warded off many false doctrines. To some people, the mere fact that equality as a social norm is relatively new is reason enough to squash it. But before we do, we need to look again at our history. Have there been times before where the church re-examined its understanding of the gospel and gained a better perspective from doing so? We don't need to think too hard to realize that the answer is yes. From Peter's ministry in Acts to the modern era, we find that the church has gained new insights many times. Let's briefly note a few of them.

We may not think about it much, but Jesus's own ministry was very new in its time. It ran counter to everything most Jewish religious experts believed. Peter and Paul both received divine guidance to open the gospel to gentiles, something that was completely without precedent in their communities. However, the Spirit led them to a better understanding, and with new eyes, they saw that this fit perfectly with the mission God had given His people since the beginning: to be a blessing to the nations. After Peter baptized Cornelius, a gentile, he went before the church in Jerusalem and had to convince them that what he had done was acceptable.

Paul spent a good deal of his ministry reiterating again and again that the gospel brought freedom from the law, while many well-meaning Christian Judaizers taught that gentiles had to first become Jews in order to be saved. Conflicts between gentile and Jewish Christians in the church persisted throughout the early church. Today, most Christians are gentiles, and we hold the freedom to meet Christ anywhere to be a fundamental element of our faith.

The Protestant Reformation was full of "new" ideas that today's evangelical world believes have always been God's ideas. The notion that any individual can come before God and commune with Him was unheard of in Martin Luther's day, as was the notion that God would or ought to speak to people by means other than the church hierarchy. For hundreds of years, only church officials could read Scripture. Religious leaders feared that if commoners had Bibles in their own language, there would be no end to misinterpretation. Vernacular Bible translations were outlawed, and many Bible translators were martyred. Yet here we stand today, reading the Bible in our own language, communing with God, and seeking the leading of the Spirit to interpret God's Word. This notion was once an abomination, though most Protestants would certainly agree that these changes were good.

Monarchy as the only feasible method of government was long justified by Scripture. After all, Jesus had said to give to Caesar what was Caesar's, and Paul had said to submit to the governing authorities, because they had been placed there by God. It was held, then, that monarchs were divinely appointed to rule, and to oppose them in any way would not just be treason against king and country, but against God. Interestingly, the first proponents of democracy were steeped in Judeo-Christian teachings (this is not to say that they were necessarily Christians) and found biblical support for their beliefs. Now, much of the world considers democracy to be at least as biblically sound as monarchy, if not more.

For many years, Europe and the Americas saw no problem with the enslavement and dehumanization of millions of Africans and later their segregation. In fact, they used the Bible to justify these actions. The same could be said of the policy of apartheid in South Africa. It was a few bold souls, many of them women, who dared to suggest that God did not support slavery and that to use the Bible to justify it was to misunderstand God's Word. It was often regular people like the former slave trader John Newton, author of "Amazing Grace," who were convicted by the Spirit to see that something was very wrong, in spite of what many thought the Bible said. Today, no Christian would argue for slavery.

Interestingly, many Christians would consider these developments to be some of the prouder moments in the church's interaction with society throughout the centuries. Yet church leaders and theologians of their day fought fiercely against these concepts. It seemed to them that Scripture speaks clearly in support of the traditional ways, and the ideas we now hold dear were new and tainted by secular culture.

Breaking with Tradition, Part 2

Theo, you are correct when you say that my beliefs about women break with tradition. The church throughout history has by and large excluded women from positions of influence over men, and this "tradition" continues to this day in many churches.

But judging from your letter to me, your beliefs about women break with tradition too! The problem is that tradition is always changing. The idea that women are "equal in value, but not in role" is not part of the historical tradition and is very much a modern tradition. In fact, it is only since the Enlightenment (starting in the 1700s) that this idea gradually became acceptable. Prior to that, people living in the Christian world were usually not considered to be of the same value and essential dignity as the nobility. Rulers were not regular people who happened to be in a powerful position. Rather, they were superior people, and that is why God had given them power. Their lives were worth more than the lives of peasants.

Likewise, between the time soon after the New Testament books were written and the 1800s, the historical tradition regarding women remained fairly consistent. With the exception of particularly devout women who were venerated, such as Saint Paula, St. Margaret of Antioch, Clotilda, Genovefa of Paris, Bishop Brigid of Kildare, Martha of Bethany, Julian of Norwich, Joan of Arc, Hilda of Whitby, and the preacher Hildegard of Bingen,[9] women were generally regarded as inferior, both in being and in role. From church fathers like Aquinas and Jerome to Calvin and Luther, and all the way up to the American Puritans and into the 1800s, there was almost uniform opposition to women being equal in value. Take a look at some quotes from well-known church fathers:

> As regards the individual nature, woman is defective and misbegotten, for the active force in the male seed tends to the production

---

9. Beth Allison Barr, *The Making of Biblical Womanhood: How the Subjugation of Women Became Gospel Truth* (Grand Rapids, MI: Brazos, 2021) 88–97.

of a perfect likeness in the masculine sex; while the production of woman comes from defect in the active force or from some material indisposition, or even from some external influence . . . So by such a kind of subjection woman is naturally subject to man, because in man the discretion of reason predominates.

> Thomas Aquinas (1225-1274), *Summa Theologica*, Volume 1, Question 92, Article 1, Replies to Objection 1 and Objection 2

For as the sun is more glorious than the moon, though the moon is a most glorious body, so woman, though she was a most beautiful work of God, yet she did not equal the glory of the male creature.

> Martin Luther (1483–1546), *Commentary on Genesis*

It is however a mistake, for Paul looks beyond this—to God's eternal law, which has made the female sex subject to the authority of men. On this account all women are born, that they may acknowledge themselves inferior in consequence of the superiority of the male sex.

> John Calvin (1509–1564), *Commentary on 1 Corinthians 11*

The second duty of the wife is constant obedience and subjection.

> John Dod, *A Plaine and Familiar Exposition of the Ten Commandements*, Puritan guidebook first published in 1603

Do not any longer contend for mastery, for power, money, or praise. Be content to be a private, insignificant person, known and loved by God and me . . . [O]f what importance is your character to mankind, if you were buried just now or if you had never lived, what loss would it be to the cause of God?

> John Wesley (1703–1791), founder of the Methodist movement, letter to his wife, July 15, 1774

Looking at what the teachers, preachers, and theologians of the historical tradition taught and comparing it to the modern traditional view, we find that they are not at all the same. In fact, just about the only thing they have in common is the belief that only men should be in leadership. The following points summarize the historical tradition regarding teachings on women:[10]

- Women are, by nature, inferior to men.

- Women are subordinated to men.

- God's design was that women should not exercise any authority in any setting, whether in public, the workplace, the church, or the home.

- Women ought to keep silent in every public or church setting.

- Women are not fully created in the image of God, but men are.

- Women are inferior and subordinated to men because they were created second chronologically.

- Women need to be subordinate to the leadership of men because they are morally weaker than men and naturally more prone to sin and deception.

And these beliefs continued through the centuries. In the 1700s, even the writers of the US Constitution only considered white, male landowners "equal." Only they could vote. For purposes of counting a state's population, the Constitution defined a black slave as only three-fifths of a person. This did not change until 1865.

The notion of people being equal in value simply by their being human is thoroughly modern. If we were to align with the teachings in church history, we would teach that women are fundamentally less valuable than men. And, sadly, this has been the mindset of religious and secular culture for most of the last 2,000 years. But when the idea of equal worth rose to popularity, it clashed with that historical tradition, giving rise to a new, quite revolutionary idea—namely that men and women are equal in value, but not in leadership, and are bound to specific roles.

---

10. The following list is adapted from Kevin Giles, *The Trinity and Subordinationism: The Doctrine of God & the Contemporary Gender Debate* (Downers Grove, IL: InterVarsity, 2002) 165–166.

So, Theo, compared to almost 2,000 years of church tradition, I am sorry to say that you and I are both radical liberals simply for believing women are as fully human as men.

But even the modern tradition is not really a tradition. This has changed significantly in the past two hundred years. I will discuss this in more detail in the next section.

Modern Christian History
Regarding Men and Women

The so-called modern tradition regarding women in the church was radically transformed during the past two hundred years. The late 1800s and early 1900s were tumultuous times in America. In this time of unprecedented change in society, a movement arose that emphasized the Holy Spirit, individual salvation, and personal morality over tradition and intellect. It ushered in new ways of understanding the place of women. This fundamentalist movement was a response to changes both in the church and in American culture.

American Protestants noticed a trend in mainline Protestantism toward increasingly liberal theology "emphasizing reason and experience over doctrinal authority."[11] The Bible and Christianity were being analyzed and picked apart by skeptical, liberal theologians and philosophers. Many American Christians perceived that an overly routine, intellectual, and regimented church had sucked the life out of the gospel. Ironically, even as they pushed back against what they perceived as secular ideology, they were influenced by it. They looked at the Bible and found justification for modern ideas like the equal worth of all people and the freedom to worship God and interpret the Bible as individuals, unfettered by the weight of church tradition.

Led by such figures as C. I. Scofield and Dwight Moody, these theologians emphasized the fundamentals of the faith and the gospel, instead of the dry, intellectual religion that was so damaging to the gospel. They preached an urgent message: Jesus was coming back, and soon. Missionaries, preachers, and evangelists were desperately needed to save as many souls as possible before Jesus returned. This movement swept the nation, particularly in the Midwest and West. Its urgency led to a greater focus on the Spirit, gifts, and conversion than on theology. Passion outweighed analysis.

---

11. https://en.wikipedia.org/wiki/Liberal_Christianity

These Fundamentalists, as they came to be called, believed that no official organized church or tradition was necessary to expose God's truth to the commoner. Putting aside formal training and church hierarchy, they distributed tracts, split into many denominations, and fanned out all over the nation. They founded Bible institutes all over the country. Many remain today, including Moody Bible Institute. They revered and believed unwaveringly in the Bible, refusing to subject it to the intellectual skepticism of university academics. Instead, they trained both men and women to share the gospel in foreign countries and at home, both in the cities and in the frontier.

In the dominant white culture of America, women had long been considered the guardians of family and morality in the home. An ideal woman did not work outside the home. This, of course, was only possible for those families with enough money. Working-class white women and women of color could not possibly live up to this ideal, but were judged by it nonetheless. Yet, women of all races and classes pushed back against cultural restrictions. It was around the beginning of the twentieth century that middle- and upper-class white women expanded their sphere of influence beyond the home and extended their role as moral guardians to society, not just family. With it, they began to gain public influence.

Meanwhile, the world in which they lived was changing as well. The industrial, often poor, urban areas were growing, leading to numerous social problems. Men, women, and children all worked long hours in factories just to feed themselves. Christian women in particular found ways to care for the poor and needy. Many united nationwide to outlaw alcohol because of its destructive impact on families. They advocated for labor unions to increase wages (ironically, so that women would not be forced to work in order for a family to survive) and limit work hours. They fought to address violence and poverty. Christian women also attended Bible institutes, preached, and evangelized all over the country. There was a bountiful harvest, but the laborers were few, and women filled the ranks.

With a progressive and changing society on one hand, and science and academia questioning the traditional understanding of Scripture on the other hand, many evangelical Christians found themselves in a corner. They responded as Christians always do to cultural movements. They accepted and adapted some things and rejected others, some consciously and others unconsciously.

Many denominations and their seminaries were considered too liberal, so those who held to the fundamentals of Christianity began to create their own institutions of higher learning. Bible institutes became colleges, universities, and seminaries. Where they had previously shunned overly academic intellectualism, they now used their own academic and intellectual prowess to defend their understanding of the Bible against outside attacks.

As they built institutions, evangelicals followed an economic trend of the time—specialization. It became less and less acceptable for only moderately trained leaders to preach and teach in churches. Just as professionals were coming into demand in industry and commerce, seminary-trained pastors became the preferred type of leader. Women were still generally unwelcome in institutions of higher learning, and the same was true of seminaries. Thus, most of the female lay preachers of the past were replaced by seminary-trained male pastors. The evangelistic fervor of the earlier years had waned, and there was less demand for woman preachers, teachers, or evangelists. Their new roles were predominantly in women's and children's ministries and foreign missions.

The work Christian women had started was taken over by others. For example, in 1871, Miss Emma Dryer, the principal and a teacher at Illinois State Normal University, began to develop a program of Bible study, teaching, and home visitation for young women. D. L. Moody persuaded her to carry on her Bible teaching under the auspices of his church. In 1883, at D. L. Moody's request, Emma Dryer organized and headed May Institute. It was renamed Moody Bible Institute after Moody died in 1899 and has continued as a private conservative evangelical Bible college ever since.

Evangelicals were arriving at a brand-new understanding of women's place in society. Like liberals, they now believed women were equal to men in worth and value. It had become acceptable for women to play some leadership role in the public sphere, something that had been almost universally unacceptable for most of church history. Where church tradition insisted that women be entirely silent in church, except for singing and saying "amen," they were now allowed to speak freely, so long as they were not exercising authority over men. Liberalism influenced them even while they consciously and publicly spoke against it.

This new view was fundamentally liberal in its belief that men and women had equal value. At the same time, it also accurately reflected the biblical account of creation, where male and female bear God's image fully. But it seemed to conflict with other Bible verses that appeared to say women should be subordinate to men. How could this tension be resolved? Two main paths emerged.

Some Christians resolved the tension by applying the modern concept of "roles" to justify women's subordination, even though the word "role" never occurs in the Bible.[12] Church tradition previously made women subordinate to men because they were inferior. The newly emerging church tradition still made women subordinate, but now on the basis that God assigned men and women different roles. Man was created with the role of leader and provider, and woman with the role of follower and nurturer. These roles aligned with what people of that era (and many people today) widely believed were men's and women's natural abilities.

According to this new view, it was okay, though not preferable, for women to work or lead outside of the church or Christian family. But because of the way a few passages in Scripture were translated, it remained unacceptable for a woman to have a leadership role in the church or to co-lead a family equally with her husband. In this new paradigm, Christians found a way to adopt

---

12. George W. Knight III, "Male and Female He Related Them," *Christianity Today* (April 9, 1976) 13–14, followed by *The Role Relationship of Men & Women: New Testament Teaching* (Chicago, IL: Moody, 1977) popularized this novel use of the word "role" from temporary to permanent "roles."

the Western culture's liberal value of equality, while also believing they were remaining faithful to the Bible and church tradition.

Other Christians took a different approach. They, too, re-examined the Bible and saw that all people were made in God's image and realized that throughout the Bible, God was always challenging his people to act in ways that empowered the oppressed and led to greater equality among people.

These Christians examined Scripture and concluded that for a variety of reasons, and in a variety of ways, we had mistranslated, misunderstood, and misapplied the Bible. They saw that God consistently used women as leaders, even though the cultures of their day opposed it. They saw that in the early church, women held many of the same leadership positions as men. They believed that when read in context, restrictions on women were intended to be temporary and applied to specific church situations. They were never meant to apply to all Christians at all times.

They concluded that the Bible supported the mutual leadership of women and men as equals in the family, in the church, and in society in general (This is my group ☺). Many of those who believed this were fundamentalist evangelical women leaders of the early twentieth century. Like many New Testament Christians before them, they broke with their cultural traditions in affirming that in Christ there is no male-female division.

If the history of women in Christianity teaches us one thing, it is that there is no single, unchanging perspective on the matter. In the Old Testament, God challenged conventional views regarding women, and Jesus and Paul did the same in the New Testament. Prevailing cultural views on a woman's value in society significantly influenced the great theologians through the centuries, as well. The last two hundred years marked a dramatic shift in views on women, resulting in these two new perspectives on the issue. Both have been influenced by culture, but apply with differing consistency the biblical insight that male and female are created equally in the image of God.

Heading into the Bible

In conclusion, Theo, men and women should live together as equals. They should use the gifts the Holy Spirit has given them, including in leading and teaching. I know many women who are extremely well-versed in the Bible. Wouldn't it be wise for me to learn from them? Or should I refuse to listen to their wisdom because they are women? I also know many women who are fantastic leaders. Should I refuse to follow their lead because they are women? No, it does not make sense to me that we should prohibit women from using their spiritual gifts in all the ways God calls them to serve, since limiting women undermines the advancement of God's kingdom.

Ultimately, however, it is totally irrelevant whether it makes sense to me. Nothing I write matters if it contradicts the Bible. Holy Scripture is the only reliable guide for knowing what God desires. If Scripture taught that God wants only men to be in charge, even though women can be great leaders, that would be the end of the discussion. God's written word trumps every ounce of human reasoning.

The trouble is that it can be hard to discern what Scripture is revealing, for numerous reasons. We are about to dig into the Bible and ask questions like, "Can a woman be a church elder?" This requires that we do our best to understand texts originally written in Greek and Hebrew. Before we do that, however, to illustrate some of the difficulties, let's consider a much simpler question: "Can a woman be president of the United States of America?" If you were studying our society from afar, what would you conclude? You would undoubtedly start by studying our Constitution, where you would find:

> The executive Power shall be vested in a President of the United States of America. He shall hold his Office during the Term of four Years, and, together with the Vice President chosen for the same Term, be elected, as follows:

From the usage of the pronouns "he" and "his," the Constitution seems to assume that the president would be a man. This use of masculine pronouns for the president is repeated over twenty times elsewhere in the Constitution, including:

> [The Bill] shall be presented to the President of the United States; and before the Same shall take Effect, shall be approved by him . . .

> The President shall, at stated Times, receive for his Services . . .

> He shall have Power, by and with the Advice and Consent of the Senate, to make Treaties . . .

However, there are also several places in the Constitution, including amendments, which are quite gender neutral, including:

> The person having the greatest Number of votes for President, shall be the President . . .

> No person shall be elected to the office of the President more than twice . . .

> [The Electors] shall name in their ballots the person voted for as President . . .

There is also the text normally used to describe the qualifications of president:

> No person except a natural born Citizen, or a Citizen of the United States, at the time of the Adoption of this Constitution, shall be eligible to the Office of President; neither shall any Person be eligible to that Office who shall not have attained to the Age of thirty-five Years, and been fourteen Years a Resident within the United States.

That seems to allow a woman to be president. However, this passage simply lists age and residency as requirements—it does not state that the list is exhaustive. Then, there is the 19th Amendment:

The right of citizens of the United States to vote shall not be denied or abridged by the United States or by any State on account of sex.

But it only mentions the right to vote, not to become president. Only men are mentioned in reference to the president; women are never mentioned in reference to the president. So maybe the Constitution is saying that only men can be president? Or maybe not?

Left with this uncertainty, you might look at actual history, and you would find that all the presidents have been men. If you looked deeper you would find women senators and representatives and, as I write this letter, a vice president, and you could argue that some of these women could become president somewhere down the chain of command, if the president became incapacitated. But this only shows that women could become president in an emergency—this doesn't necessarily include being voted into office (and maybe the transfer of power would pass over her).

There have been several women who have run for president, so you might think that means that women could become president. And it probably does, but all we have so far is the fact that the courts have not tried to disqualify them based on their gender. And a "lack of a negative court opinion" hardly seems like a strong argument.

My point is that for this question, the answer should be easy. This is a question about our culture, all the documents are in English, and we even know the answer. Yes! Of course, a woman can be president of the United States! But nowhere is it stated unequivocally that this is the case. The Constitution seems to talk with two voices—one voice assuming that all presidents were going to be men, but the other voice allowing for the possibility that someday things may change.

We have a similar issue when figuring out what the Bible says about women in leadership. When it comes to the Bible, however, we are not part of the societies in question, none of the original documents are in English, and we don't come into this process already knowing the answer. Our task then becomes much, much harder. The Bible is a book of history—and that history is filled with leadership that is predominantly male. But the Bible is also a book of inspiration and revelation. Somehow, we must separate "God's desire for how we should live" from "What God has allowed to happen in the past."

So, in the following sections, I will look at every relevant Bible passage and attempt to show how Scripture itself teaches that men and women should serve alongside each other as equals, not in a hierarchy of man over woman.

For each passage I discuss, scholars have written many books and articles about the possible nuances of that passage. I won't try to discuss them all. That would make this letter far too long and confusing. Rather, for each passage, I will give the best explanation I can find and simplify it as much as possible to show you how the passage's plain text (with some Greek and Hebrew explanation thrown in) points to God's heart for men and women serving together as equals.

If you want to explore any of the Biblical analysis further, I recommend two other sources for you to look at:

- Philip B. Payne's book, *Man and Woman, One in Christ.*[13] At the beginning of each section, I have added a footnote with corresponding pages from that book, where you can find much greater detail.

- CBE International. Its website (**www.cbeinternational.org**) has an enormous number of resources available, including articles, videos, and books by many different authors.

Theo, I encourage you to follow along with your Bible as well as Greek and Hebrew interlinear versions. You can find them online, or use the excellent, free Bible software "E-Sword" (**www.e-sword.net**). This way, you can confirm for yourself all the points I make and be satisfied that what I write is grounded in Scripture. With that said, let's go ahead and dive into the Bible to see what it says.

---

13. Philip B. Payne, *Man and Woman, One in Christ: An Exegetical and Theological Study of Paul's Letters*, Grand Rapids, MI: Zondervan, 2009, 40% off at https://www.linguistsoftware.com/manandwoman.htm.

Part Two

OLD TESTAMENT PASSAGES

Genesis 1 & 2: Creation of Man and Woman[14]

Okay, Theo, now we can start digging into the Bible! I am sure you want to jump to the "fun" verses of Paul, but I will just go in biblical order, starting with Genesis. You can feel free to skip ahead to passages that are most important to you. But let me start by stating clearly that I believe that the original text of the Bible, properly translated and interpreted, affirms the shared leadership, authority, and gifting of both men and women. This starts in Genesis, where the creation story presents the equal standing of men and women as God's original design.

Genesis 1 presents a grand overview of the whole of creation, culminating with the creation of man and woman with the same blessing and authority. Their equality in God's image and in rule over the earth is evident in the words that are plural, highlighted in bold below:

> Then God said, "Let us make mankind in our image, in our likeness, so that **they** may **rule** over the fish in the sea and the birds in the sky, over the livestock and all the wild animals, and over all the creatures that move along the ground." So God created mankind in his own image, in the image of God he created **them; male and female** he created **them**. God blessed **them** and said to **them**, "**Be fruitful** and **increase** in number; **fill** the earth and **subdue** it. **Rule** over the fish in the sea and the birds in the sky and over every living creature that moves on the ground." Then God said, "I give **you** every seed-bearing plant on the face of the whole earth and every tree that has fruit with

---

14. For further discussion, see Payne, *Man and Woman, One in Christ*, 41–47.

*seed in it. They will be **yours** for food."* . . . *And it was so* . . . *and it was very good.* (Genesis 1:26–31)

Throughout this passage, you can see that man and woman are treated equally:

- God creates both male and female in God's image and likeness (1:26–27).

- God gives both male and female rule over all the animals of the earth (1:26, 28).

- God gives both male and female the same blessing and tells them together to be fruitful and increase in number, fill the earth, and subdue it (1:28), mentioning no distinction in roles.

- God speaks directly to both man and woman (1:28–29 to "them," to "you" plural twice).

- God gives male and female together all plants for food (1:29 "you," "yours" plural).

Genesis 2 gives more details about the creation of man and woman:

The LORD God said, "It is not good for the man to be alone. I will make a helper suitable for him." Now the LORD God had formed out of the ground all the wild animals and all the birds in the sky. He brought them to the man to see what he would name them; and whatever the man called each living creature, that was its name. So the man gave names to all the livestock, the birds in the sky and all the wild animals. But for Adam no suitable helper was found. So the LORD God caused the man to fall into a deep sleep; and while he was sleeping, he took one of the man's ribs and then closed up the place with flesh. Then the LORD God made a woman from the rib he had taken out of the man, and he brought her to the man. The man said, "This is now bone of my bones and flesh of my flesh; she shall be called 'woman,' for she was taken out of man." (Genesis 2:18–23)

In contrast to the refrain *"it was good"* for every other stage of creation, God declares, *"It is not good for the man to be alone."* Theo, stop and notice that this gives the original purpose of woman: to be a friend and companion to man. Man's need is not for an assistant—he does not need help removing thorns and thistles from the garden (see 3:18) or mending his clothes (because he doesn't have any!). What he needs is companionship. He is alone. God creates woman so he will not be alone.

The woman is described as *"a helper suitable for him."* The Hebrew text here is *'ezer knegdo*. The first word, *'ezer,* can be translated "helper," which unfortunately in English implies a subordinate or servant. Never in the Bible, however, does the word *'ezer* suggest "helper" as in "servant," but almost always (sixteen times) it refers to God, acting as his people's rescuer, strength, or might. For example:

> [One son] *was named Eliezer, for he said, "My father's God was my helper* ('ezer); *he saved me from the sword of Pharaoh."* (Exodus 18:4).

> *All you Israelites, trust in the LORD—he is their help* ('ezer) *and shield.* (Psalm 115:9).

> *You are destroyed, Israel, because you are against me, against your helper* ('ezer). (Hosea 13:9).

And in the three times *'ezer* does not describe God, it describes a military protector. Theo, if you were just reading all the uses of *'ezer* in the Bible, there is no way you would ever think it was referring to an assistant or any other kind of subordinate helper. Nothing in the context of any of these passages suggests that, as *'ezer,* either God or woman is subordinate to man. So, a better translation of this word is "strength."

The second word, *knegdo,* contains three parts: *k* ("as") + *negd* ("in front of") + *o* ("him") and so conveys "as in front of him." Therefore, *'ezer knegdo,* is better translated as "a strength corresponding to him." Nothing in the expression *'ezer knegdo* in Genesis 2 implies that God created woman as a subordinate helper for man. Quite the opposite—it highlights her strength to be an equal partner with man and one rescuing him from being alone. She is his counterpart: his companion and friend, who along with him rules over the earth. She fulfills him so that together they can be fruitful and care for the earth.

This detailed Genesis account of the creation of man and woman also consistently emphasizes their equality. God makes woman from the man's rib, and the man recognizes *"This is now bone of my bones and flesh of my flesh"* (2:23) because they share the same substance (2:21–23). *"Father and mother"* are identified without hierarchical distinction (2:24). In marriage, they are *"united"* and *"one flesh"* (2:24). Both are naked and feel no shame; they share moral innocence (2:25).

GENESIS 1 & 2: ANSWERS TO COMMON OBJECTIONS

That said, I know you may share three common objections, often stated as follows:

> **"God presents woman to man, and man names her 'woman' (Genesis 2:23). This act of naming implies that man has authority over woman."**

Okay, I will agree that there is a correlation between authority and naming rights. However, this correlation does not go both ways; giving something a name does not mean you have authority over it. The authority must come first. For example, when God says, *"Let there be light"* (Genesis 1:3) or *"Let us make mankind in our image"* (1:26), as Creator, he has authority over his creation and that includes "naming rights." Similarly, parents name the children they create. But the man created nothing. God created woman from one of the man's ribs, and the man slept through the whole thing! It was God's right to name all the creatures, and God allowed the man to have the honor of doing so. But even though the man named the animals (2:20), the text does not say that included giving the man more authority over the animals than the woman had. On the contrary, God repeatedly gives the authority over creation to both the man and the woman equally (1:26, 28, 29).

But, Theo, I want you to notice that in this verse, the man does not name her at all. He does not assign any personal name until Genesis 3:20, when he names her "Eve." As God brought all the animals to him, the man was not giving them personal names like Fluffy, Fido, or Bambi, rather he was distinguishing different kinds of creatures, such as cat, dog, deer, and so on. And when the Lord brought his newest creation to the man, he recognized her and exclaimed, *"This is now bone of my bones and flesh of my flesh; she shall be called 'woman,' for she was taken out of man"* (2:23). The word used for "woman" is not some Hebrew word or phrase that means "taken out of man." The Hebrew word *'ishah,* meaning "woman," is simply the word for man, *'ish,* with a feminine ending. Because Hebrew is one of those languages that has different endings for masculine and feminine forms of the same word, it sounds like a completely different word. But it is not. Nor is it a personal name. The point of his exclamation was that he recognized this new creation as his female counterpart, hence his joyous, "at last!" in 2:23. He exclaims, "She is human like me, my female counterpart, so she shall be called *'ishah,* 'female human'!"

Finally, you should realize that the man only names the woman "Eve" *after the Fall* (Genesis 3:20).

"Man was created first. That implies that man has authority over woman."

Nowhere does Genesis indicate that creation-order implies a hierarchy of authority. For example, animals created on the fifth day do not have authority over animals created on the sixth day, nor do any of them have authority over man and woman, who were created later. And regarding humans, in spite of the Near Eastern custom of giving preference to firstborn sons, God almost always subverts this custom at crucial junctures: God chose Abel's sacrifice over Cain's, made his covenant with Isaac over Ishmael, blessed Jacob over Esau, blessed Joseph over his older brothers, blessed Ephraim over Manasseh, blessed Perez over Zerah in the line of Christ, blessed Moses over Aaron, blessed David over his seven older brothers, blessed Solomon over Adonijah.

In the text, the creation of woman later highlights man's need for a partner corresponding to him. It says nothing about man's being created first somehow giving man authority over woman. Genesis says nothing about an order of creation in the sense of a hierarchy of authority, with authority given to the one created first.

> **"But later in the Bible, in 1 Corinthians 11 and again in 1 Timothy 2, Paul talks about the creation of man and woman in Genesis, and he shows how the creation story demonstrates the leadership role of men and the submissive role of women."**

Actually, no he does not. Not at all. But that is skipping ahead too far. I will get to those verses later.

Genesis 3: The Fall[15]

Genesis 3 describes the Fall. Genesis 3:1–5 narrates the conversation in which "the serpent" addresses the woman. Then the woman and man decide to disobey God and eat the forbidden fruit:

> *When the woman saw that the fruit of the tree was good for food and pleasing to the eye, and also desirable for gaining wisdom, she took some and ate it. She also gave some to her husband, who was with her, and he ate it.* (Genesis 3:6)

Because they disobeyed God's command, God punishes the serpent, the woman, and the man. Because she disobeyed his command, God addresses the woman directly in verse 13, saying, "*What is this you have done?*"

The woman receives bad news:

> *To the woman he said, "I will make your pains in childbearing very severe; with painful labor you will give birth to children. Your desire will be for your husband, and he will rule over you."* (Genesis 3:16)

The phrase "*desire will be for*" in Genesis 3:16 is rare. It sounds like a good thing, doesn't it? It sounds like she will deeply love her husband. But we can discern its actual meaning from the closest parallel usage in Genesis 4:7 about Cain: "*sin is crouching at your door; it desires to have you, but you must rule over it.*" Sin desired to have Cain, which meant that sin desired to master or manipulate Cain. Similarly, the phrase "*your desire will be for your husband*" means that the woman's desire will be "to master, control, or manipulate your husband." There is nothing loving about that! The Fall had transformed the relationship of Adam and Eve from ruling over God's creation side by side, into a fierce power struggle with each one trying to

---

15. For further discussion, see Payne, *Man and Woman, One in Christ*, 47–54.

rule the other. God states the consequences of her sin, concluding in verse 16, *"and he will rule over you."*

All the other effects of the Fall are clearly contrary to and distortions of God's intent in creation. It would be out of harmony with every other consequence of the Fall to interpret man's rule over woman as something good that should be fostered. Everything in Genesis 3:14–19 is disastrous news for the person addressed, and every other result of the Fall for humankind is something people should try to overcome, such as pain in childbearing (through medical or relaxation techniques) and removal of thorns and thistles (through weeding and farming). People should strive to overcome—rather than foster—the consequences of the Fall, including the husband's rule over his wife and the wife's desire to rule over her husband.

Finally, notice the equality of man and woman throughout this chapter. Together, they face temptation and disobey God's command (3:6). They both realize they are naked and sew coverings (3:7). Both hide from God (3:8), showing they were both ashamed that they had disobeyed God. Both blame someone else (3:12–13). God speaks directly to both, announcing specific consequences resulting from their sin (3:9–13, 16–19). And in the end, both are personally responsible for their own disobedience.

GENESIS 3: ANSWERS TO COMMON OBJECTIONS

As before, there are several common objections to the equality of men and women in this chapter.

> **"When the man and woman are hiding, God calls out man first, asking 'Where are you?' This implies that the man spoke for both of them."**

Genesis 3:13 clearly states, *"Then the Lord God said to the woman, 'What is this you have done?' The woman said, 'The serpent deceived me, and I ate.'"* The man did not speak for her. The Bible never explains why God called the man first. Maybe it was simply because the man was the first one to be told *"you must not eat from the tree of the knowledge of good and evil"* (2:17). Or maybe it was to mirror the order of the Fall: the serpent spoke to the woman, who gave the fruit to her husband, and he ate it. Then that order is reversed: God speaks to the man, then the woman, then the serpent. But this is all speculation. Nothing in the text implies that men should have greater authority and responsibility than women.

> **"God created man to rule over woman. When God says, 'he shall rule over you,' he is talking only about oppressive rule, not God-designed leadership."**

If you search your Bible for the Hebrew word used here for "rule," you will find that it simply means "rule." The word itself does not imply bad rule. Both major Hebrew dictionaries analyze every Old Testament instance of this word used for rule and list no negative meaning for it. For example, the Hebrew word is used in these verses as well:

> *Joseph said, "God . . . made me . . . **ruler** of all Egypt."* (Genesis 45:8)

> *Sihon king of the Amorites, who reigned in Heshbon. He **ruled** from Aroer on the rim of the Arnon Gorge—from the middle of the gorge— to the Jabbok River, which is the border of the Ammonites. This included half of Gilead.* (Joshua 12:2)

> *The Israelites said to Gideon, "**Rule** over us—you, your son and your grandson—because you have saved us from the hand of Midian."* (Judges 8:22)

> *dominion belongs to the LORD and he **rules** over the nations.* (Psalm 22:28)

Additionally, virtually all Bibles translate this verb as future: "*he **will** rule over you.*" Like all the other results of the Fall, it identifies something new and contrary to God's original creation design. This means that before this point in time, man was not ruling over woman. Genesis 3:16 simply identifies man's rule over woman—not oppressive rule—as the new state that resulted from her disobedience. Man's rule over woman is itself contrary to God's original plan of man and woman ruling over the earth together.

"Adam is faulted 'because he listened to his wife.'"

Genesis 3:17 says that God cursed the ground *"Because you listened to your wife and ate fruit from the tree about which I commanded you, 'You must not eat from it.'"* Some people read into this that Adam "abandoned his leadership" and "this moral failure led to his ruination." However, in this case, the only reason it was wrong for Adam to listen to his wife was that she was offering him what God had prohibited. God responds in this way specifically because Adam blamed *"The woman you put here with me"* (3:12) for his eating the fruit. God highlights Adam's sins of disobedience and blaming the woman and, implicitly, blaming God who put her there! If the fruit had been from any other tree, it would not have been a sin for the man to listen to his wife and eat.

Deborah: God's Chosen Leader[16]

Theo, consider the story of Deborah, one of the early leaders of Israel. Deborah was one of the judges "the Lord raised up" who "saved them out of the hands of their enemies" (Judges 2:16, 18; 4:10, 14, 24; 5:1–31). She was a prophet and the highest leader in all of Israel. Observe the straightforward manner in which the Bible introduces Deborah:

> *Now Deborah, a prophet, the wife of Lappidoth, was leading Israel at that time. She held court under the Palm of Deborah between Ramah and Bethel in the hill country of Ephraim, and the Israelites went up to her to have their disputes decided. (Judges 4:4–5)*

Notice that the text makes no suggestion whatsoever that anything was amiss because this judge, Deborah, was a woman or that she had any obligation to defer to her husband. She was simply the leader of Israel and people came to her for judgment.

Furthermore, she, a wife and mother (5:7), had the authority to command Barak, Israel's military commander "Go" (4:6, 14), resulting in their successful defeat of Jabin's army. They worked together well with shared authority: he as a military commander, she as commander in chief. For his action, Barak was commended in Hebrews:

> *And what more shall I say? I do not have time to tell about Gideon, Barak, Samson and Jephthah, about David and Samuel and the prophets, who through faith conquered kingdoms, administered justice, and gained what was promised; who shut the mouths of lions, quenched the fury of the flames, and escaped the edge of the sword; whose weakness was turned to strength; and who became powerful in battle and routed foreign armies. (Hebrews 11:32–34)*

---

16. For further discussion, see Payne, *Man and Woman, One in Christ*, 55–56.

And Israel was blessed because of her leadership:

> *Then the land had peace forty years.* (Judges 5:31)

The story of Deborah and Barak powerfully demonstrates God's use of female leadership.

DEBORAH: ANSWERS TO COMMON OBJECTIONS

As simple and straightforward as the narrative of Deborah is, the following objections have been raised about using Deborah as evidence that God approves of female leaders:

> **"During this time, Israel was enslaved after worshipping false gods and the people were completely corrupt. No man could be found to lead, so Deborah became the leader. Since all the other judges in the Bible were men, God clearly prefers men to lead."**

The idea that God could not find a man to lead may at first glance appear plausible. After all, many of the male Old Testament leaders were extremely reluctant to lead. Moses refused repeatedly to lead Israel, coming up with excuse after excuse. Similarly, God told Gideon, the judge immediately after Deborah, to go lead Israel, and Gideon came up with excuse after excuse. However, God was willing and able to "shock and awe" both of them to become Israel's leader. Moses finally agreed only after God performed many signs and wonders for him and allowed him to take his brother, Aaron, along to do the speaking. Similarly, Gideon ultimately agreed only after extensive negotiations with God and witnessing signs and wonders. In this story, we know that Barak was a willing leader who only needed a little prompting to lead his troops into battle. Surely God could have convinced Barak to be Israel's judge if God had wanted to. Deborah was the leader of Israel because God chose her to lead Israel, not because God tried to get a male leader but failed and had to settle for a woman.

> "Because of the awful circumstances that Israel was in at the time, we should not take Deborah's leadership as a normal example. It was a one-time exception for exceptional times."

In reality, the times were not that exceptional. Yes, Israel had been enslaved by the Canaanites. But Israel had been enslaved before by the Egyptians. Then Israel was in the desert for forty years (Exodus 16:35). Israel had already been enslaved two other times in Judges before Deborah, and they would be enslaved many other times after Deborah. The period of kings followed, with a few good kings and many horrible, awful kings. There was nothing particularly exceptional about the specific time period during which Deborah was chosen by God to lead Israel. And as mentioned above, if God had wanted a man to lead Israel, then God's desire would not have been thwarted.

> "Every other judge before and after Deborah was 'raised up' by God to deliver Israel militarily from their enemies. Deborah was not a military leader. Barak was the military leader who delivered Israel, not Deborah."

Theo, which is easier: (1) To lead your troops into a single battle in which God has already guaranteed victory and drawn up the battle plans, or (2) To lead a sinful, rebellious nation into forty years of peace? Give Barak credit for trusting Deborah with his life and the lives of his men and going into battle. Deborah, however, is the exceptional leader here.

> "Because Barak asked Deborah (a woman) to accompany him into battle, he was denied the honor of killing the commander of the enemy forces—the honor went to a woman instead. This demonstrates that it was a sign of weakness for him to ask a woman to join him. He should have just 'been a man' and led his troops by himself."

I agree that when Deborah told Barak that God wanted him to lead his troops into battle, the best response would have been for Barak to go directly without question. Had he done that, Judges 4:9 seems to imply that he would have been able to kill Sisera himself and get the honor that goes with it. However, that honor went instead to Jael, the wife of Heber (Judges 4:21). But in the end, Barak's eventual willingness to obey Deborah resulted in Barak's army being successful, Israel being freed, Deborah's song praising Barak (Judges 5:12), and his name being written in the legion of honor found in the book of Hebrews. So, the supposed honor Barak lost due to his initial demand that Deborah accompany him in battle was tiny in comparison to the larger honor of ultimately obeying God. A key thing for us to learn from this passage is that when a prophet gives a message from God to go, we should go, whether the prophet is a man or a woman.

> **"Given Israel's decrepit spiritual state at the time, we should not understand Judges as illustrating God's ideal—God was simply working with the people he had."**

Yes, the Israelites repeatedly disobeyed God's judges. However, nothing in the description of Deborah implies that she was not God's first choice or was somehow second best. She is the one judge that is not rebuked, only praised, throughout Scripture. This pattern is also evident regarding Judah's and Israel's kings, whom we consider next.

Kings and Priests: Male Only?[17]

Let me digress a bit to consider God's leadership plan for Israel. Some of those previous objections assumed that God prefers male leaders, so let us consider the two major types of leaders in the Old Testament: kings and priests. Even though there are not that many judges, the book of Judges does, indeed, reflect God's ideal leadership structure, with the judges guiding Israel under God, the true king. It was God who was supposed to be our king; we were not supposed to have human kings. But the people revolted and demanded a king, so God relented as 1 Samuel records:

> And the LORD told him [Samuel]: "Listen to all that the people are saying to you; it is not you they have rejected, but they have rejected me as their king. As they have done from the day I brought them up out of Egypt until this day, forsaking me and serving other gods, so they are doing to you. Now listen to them; but warn them solemnly and let them know what the king who will reign over them will claim as his rights." (1 Samuel 8:7–9)

Judges were God's original design. However, God worked with humans to give them the leaders they demanded.

What about priests? God did assign the priesthood to Aaron and his sons (Numbers 18:1–7). The Bible does not give a reason for this, but we know this was not God's long-term plan. The Old Testament ideal was for the entire people of Israel to be "a kingdom of priests and a holy nation":

> Then Moses went up to God, and the LORD called to him from the mountain and said, "This is what you are to say to the descendants of Jacob and what you are to tell the people of Israel: 'You yourselves have seen what I did to Egypt, and how I carried you on eagles' wings and brought you to myself. Now if you obey me fully and keep my

17. For further discussion, see Payne, *Man and Woman, One in Christ*, 55.

covenant, then out of all nations you will be my treasured possession. Although the whole earth is mine, you will be for me a kingdom of priests and a holy nation.' These are the words you are to speak to the Israelites." (Exodus 19:3–6)

Also, Isaiah 61:6 predicts a future when all God's people *"will be called priests of the Lord, you will be named ministers of our God."*

And ultimately, God brought about the priesthood of all his people in the New Testament church:

> *But you are a chosen people, a royal priesthood, a holy nation, God's special possession, that you may declare the praises of him who called you out of darkness into his wonderful light.* (1 Peter 2:9)

So, there you have it—kings were not God's first choice; judges were. God did establish male priests of the sons of Aaron. But now Jesus is our high priest, so there is no need for any other intercessory priest. We are all priests with a direct connection to God!

Proverbs 31: An Excellent Wife[18]

The most extensive Bible passage on the position of a wife and her activities is the description of an excellent wife in Proverbs 31:10–31:

> *A wife of noble character who can find? She is worth far more than rubies.*
> *Her husband has full confidence in her and lacks nothing of value.*
> *She brings him good, not harm, all the days of her life.*
> *She selects wool and flax and works with eager hands.*
> *She is like the merchant ships, bringing her food from afar.*
> *She gets up while it is still night; she provides food for her family and portions for her female servants.*
> *She considers a field and buys it; out of her earnings she plants a vineyard.*
> *She sets about her work vigorously; her arms are strong for her tasks.*
> *She sees that her trading is profitable, and her lamp does not go out at night.*
> *In her hand she holds the distaff and grasps the spindle with her fingers.*
> *She opens her arms to the poor and extends her hands to the needy.*
> *When it snows, she has no fear for her household;*
> *for all of them are clothed in scarlet.*
> *She makes coverings for her bed; she is clothed in fine linen and purple.*
> *Her husband is respected at the city gate,*
> *where he takes his seat among the elders of the land.*
> *She makes linen garments and sells them,*
> *and supplies the merchants with sashes.*
> *She is clothed with strength and dignity; she can laugh at the days to come.*
> *She speaks with wisdom, and faithful instruction is on her tongue.*
> *She watches over the affairs of her household*
> *and does not eat the bread of idleness.*
> *Her children arise and call her blessed; her husband also, and he praises her:*
> *"Many women do noble things, but you surpass them all."*
> *Charm is deceptive, and beauty is fleeting;*
> *but a woman who fears the LORD is to be praised.*

18. For further discussion, see Payne, *Man and Woman, One in Christ*, 54–55.

Honor her for all her hands have done,
and let her works bring her praise at the city gate.

So, what characterizes this idealized "wife of noble character"? She:

- is an efficient executive with a well-ordered domestic staff
- deals in real estate
- runs a clothing business
- cares for the poor as well as her own household
- has her own earnings
- appears to be the primary income earner in the family
- is a wise and kind teacher

Theo, does this line up with your beliefs about the roles of women?

Female Leadership in the Old Testament[19]

We have discussed Deborah, but the Old Testament also praises many other women—including wives and mothers—who exercised leadership over men. It describes these women in leadership with God's blessing, with no hint that their gender should disqualify them. For example, the prophetess Miriam is sent by God "to lead" Israel:

> *I brought you up out of Egypt and redeemed you from the land of slavery. I sent Moses to lead you, also Aaron and Miriam.* (Micah 6:4)

Unlike the Bible's criticism of every king of Israel and Judah, the Bible praises but gives no criticism of these three queens: Queen Esther who used her influence to save the Jews from annihilation (Esther 7:1–10; 9:1–32), the Queen of Sheba (1 Kings 10:1–13; 2 Chronicles 9:1–12), and the Queen of Chaldea (Daniel 5:10–12). So, it would be a mistake to think that male kings in the Bible prove that God desires or praises only male leadership. Furthermore, the records of the kings of Judah always note or name the queen mothers (cf. Jeremiah 13:18; 29:2; 2 Kings 24:15). They included Bathsheba (1 Kings 2:17–19), Maacah (1 Kings 15:2, 10, 13), and Nehushta (2 Kings 24:8).

In the English language, we use completely different words for "king" and "queen," which makes it appear that kings are distinct from queens. However, Theo, you should know that in Hebrew and other Semitic languages both the word for "king" and the word for "queen" are noun forms of the verb "to rule" (*malak*). The word for "queen," *malkah,* is the feminine form of the word for "king."

Additionally, priests consulted the prophetess Huldah on finding the lost book of the law and submitted to her spiritual leadership. Israel's leaders, including the king, the elders, the prophets, and the people, accepted her word as divinely revealed (2 Kings 22:14–23:3; 2 Chronicles 34:22–32). The obedience

---

19. For further discussion, see Payne, *Man and Woman, One in Christ,* 55–57.

of Israel's male leadership to God's word spoken through her sparked what is probably the greatest revival in the history of Israel (2 Kings 22:14–23:25; 2 Chronicles 34:29–35:19).

Nothing in the Old Testament says that God permitted women to hold such political or religious authority over men only because of special circumstances, nor are those cases described as exceptions to a scriptural principle. Although two female monarchs of Israel, Athaliah (2 Kings 11:1–3; 2 Chronicles 22:10–12) and Jezebel (1 Kings 18:4), were wicked, so were most of Israel's kings. Scripture does not criticize them or any other woman leader of Israel on the grounds that women should not have authority over men. Instead, the Old Testament presents women in religious and political leadership as normal. Some are explicitly stated to have been raised up by God and blessed.

Indeed, Old Testament prophets revealed God's intentions for a greater prophetic role for women. Moses wished that all of God's people were prophets:

> *A young man ran and told Moses, "Eldad and Medad are prophesying in the camp." Joshua son of Nun, who had been Moses' aide since youth, spoke up and said, "Moses, my lord, stop them!" But Moses replied, "Are you jealous for my sake? I wish that all the LORD's people were prophets and that the LORD would put his Spirit on them!"* (Numbers 11:27–29)

Later on, Joel echoed that desire:

> *And afterward, I will pour out my Spirit on all people. Your sons and daughters will prophesy, your old men will dream dreams, your young men will see visions. Even on my servants, both men and women, I will pour out my Spirit in those days.* (Joel 2:28–20)

And as you know, this wonderful promise was fulfilled at Pentecost:

> *Then Peter stood up with the Eleven, raised his voice and addressed the crowd: "Fellow Jews and all of you who live in Jerusalem, let me*

explain this to you; listen carefully to what I say. These people are not drunk, as you suppose. It's only nine in the morning! No, this is what was spoken by the prophet Joel:

> *In the last days, God says,*
> > *"I will pour out my Spirit on all people.*
>
> *Your sons and daughters will prophesy,*
> > *your young men will see visions,*
> > *your old men will dream dreams.*
>
> *Even on my servants, both men and women,*
> > *I will pour out my Spirit in those days,*
> > *and they will prophesy.*
>
> *I will show wonders in the heavens above*
> > *and signs on the earth below,*
> > *blood and fire and billows of smoke.*
>
> *The sun will be turned to darkness*
> > *and the moon to blood*
> > *before the coming of the great and glorious day of the Lord.*
>
> *And everyone who calls*
> > *on the name of the Lord will be saved."* (Acts 2:14–21)

Finally, God even used women in the greatest of all prophetic roles: speaking key portions of inspired Scripture. These include the songs of Miriam (Exodus 15:21) and Deborah (Judges 5:2–31), Hannah's prayer (1 Samuel 2:1–10), and the *"inspired utterance"* of King Lemuel's mother (Proverbs 31:1–31). Peeking ahead in the New Testament, God continued to speak through women in this way through the Song of Elizabeth (Luke 1:25, 42–45) and Mary's Magnificat, which is the first Christian exposition of Scripture (Luke 1:46–55). Quite the opposite of excluding women from leadership over men, God appointed women to both secular and sacred leadership.

Part Three
New Testament Passages

Jesus's Treatment of Women[20]

At last, Theo, we have made it to the New Testament! Let me start by talking about how Jesus interacted with women.

> *For whoever does the will of my Father in heaven is my brother and sister and mother.* (Matthew 12:50)

As in this affirmation, Jesus in all his words and deeds left us an example to treat women as equals with men, never subordinated or restricted in role. His treatment of women as equals defied the judicial, cultural, and religious customs of his day.

When it came to judicial matters, women's rights were widely limited, such as those regarding adultery and divorce. For example, first-century Palestinian Jewish women, in general, could not divorce their husbands, but husbands could divorce their wives. Jesus, however, taught his disciples to treat husbands and wives equally:

> *He answered, "Anyone who divorces his wife and marries another woman commits adultery against her. And if she divorces her husband and marries another man, she commits adultery."* (Mark 10:11–12)

This was such a controversial teaching that the disciples had problems accepting it:

---

20. For further discussion, see Payne, *Man and Woman, One in Christ*, 57–59.

> *The disciples said to him, "If this is the situation between a husband and wife, it is better not to marry." (Matthew 19:10)*

Regarding cultural issues, women were generally regarded as intellectually and morally inferior to men. Jesus, however, respected women's intelligence and spiritual capacity, as is evident in the spiritual truths he taught to women such as the Samaritan woman (John 4:10–26) and Martha (John 11:25–26). Jesus defied convention in welcoming the support of women who left their homes and families to travel with him and his other disciples:

> *After this, Jesus traveled about from one town and village to another, proclaiming the good news of the kingdom of God. The Twelve were with him, and also some women who had been cured of evil spirits and diseases: Mary (called Magdalene) from whom seven demons had come out; Joanna the wife of Chuza, the manager of Herod's household; Susanna; and many others. These women were helping to support them out of their own means. (Luke 8:1–3)*

As for religious customs, the religious education of women was frowned upon. Jesus, however, encouraged women to be his disciples. For example, when Mary *"sat at the Lord's feet listening to what he said"* (Luke 10:39), she was taking the posture and position of a disciple. When Martha told Jesus that she wanted her sister Mary to stop learning at Jesus's feet as a disciple and come help her out, Jesus replied, *"Mary has chosen what is better, and it will not be taken away from her"* (Luke 10:42). It is generally agreed that disciples in Jesus's day were trained to carry on a rabbi's teachings, typically becoming teachers themselves.

In contrast to the rabbis teaching only male disciples, Jesus taught both men and women. This implies that he wanted women as well as men to be religious teachers. Furthermore, Jesus did not prevent women from proclaiming the gospel to men. He encouraged them! After all, the first Christian missionary was a Samaritan woman: *"Many of the Samaritans from that town believed in him because of the woman's testimony"* (John 4:39; 28–42). Also, the first person the resurrected Christ sought out and commissioned to announce the gospel of his resurrection and his coming ascension to God the Father was Mary Magdalene (John 20:14–18).

Yet Jesus chose only men as his original twelve disciples. Does this mean that he thereby excluded women from church leadership? No. Simply choosing men for the twelve apostles does not logically exclude women from church leadership any more than his choosing free Jews for the twelve apostles excludes gentiles or slaves from church leadership. Besides, Paul calls Junia *"outstanding among the apostles"* (Roman 16:7).

So, why did Jesus choose all men and no women for the original twelve apostles? Although the New Testament does not explain his reasons, Jesus probably chose men for two reasons: to avoid scandal and to symbolize the "new Israel." If Jesus had included women in gatherings in the shadow of darkness, especially in the wilderness or in places like the garden of Gethsemane, this would have raised moral suspicions not only about Jesus, but also about these twelve, on whose integrity the church would depend. Furthermore, Jesus's appointment of twelve Jewish free men paralleled the twelve sons of Israel and reinforced the symbolism of the church as the "new Israel" (Matthew 19:28; Luke 22:30; Revelation 21:12–14).

As you know, Theo, as Christians we strive to be more like Jesus in all things. We should follow his example and follow his teachings, including how he related to women. Since Christ treated women as equal to men and respected their intelligence to handle even the deepest truths, we should too.

Acts 4: Ananias and Sapphira[21]

The story of Ananias and Sapphira has some important implications. Acts narrates the infilling of the Holy Spirit that marks the beginning of the new Christian community and Peter's speech at Pentecost. All of them were filled with the Holy Spirit, striving to live according to God's ideals:

> After they prayed, the place where they were meeting was shaken. And they were all filled with the Holy Spirit and spoke the word of God boldly. All the believers were one in heart and mind. No one claimed that any of their possessions was their own, but they shared everything they had. With great power the apostles continued to testify to the resurrection of the Lord Jesus. And God's grace was so powerfully at work in them all that there were no needy persons among them. For from time to time those who owned land or houses sold them, brought the money from the sales and put it at the apostles' feet, and it was distributed to anyone who had need. Joseph, a Levite from Cyprus, whom the apostles called Barnabas (which means "son of encouragement"), sold a field he owned and brought the money and put it at the apostles' feet. (Acts 4:31–37)

Alas, it was not long before sin entered this vibrant community:

> Now a man named Ananias, together with his wife Sapphira, also sold a piece of property. With his wife's full knowledge he kept back part of the money for himself, but brought the rest and put it at the apostles' feet. Then Peter said, "Ananias, how is it that Satan has so filled your heart that you have lied to the Holy Spirit and have kept for yourself some of the money you received for the land? Didn't it belong to you before it was sold? And after it was sold, wasn't the money at your disposal? What made you think of doing such a thing? You have not lied just to human beings but to God." When Ananias heard this, he

---

21. For further discussion, see Payne, *Man and Woman, One in Christ*, 131.

fell down and died. And great fear seized all who heard what had hap-
pened. Then some young men came forward, wrapped up his body,
and carried him out and buried him. (Acts 5:1–6)

Ananias lied about his gift to the community and died for his transgression.
He was the one who brought in the offering, so his guilt was obvious. But Sapphira's guilt is not so clear—so Peter questioned her. Observe what happened
when Peter interviewed her without her husband present:

About three hours later his wife came in, not knowing what had hap-
pened. Peter asked her, "Tell me, is this the price you and Ananias got
for the land?" "Yes," she said, "that is the price." Peter said to her, "How
could you conspire to test the Spirit of the Lord? Listen! The feet of the
men who buried your husband are at the door, and they will carry you
out also." At that moment she fell down at his feet and died. Then the
young men came in and, finding her dead, carried her out and buried
her beside her husband. (Acts 5:7–10)

From the evidence of her dead body, I think it's clear she gave the wrong
answer. We have to guess a little bit at what the right answer was, but I think
it is safe to say that the right answer was to tell the truth. She was supposed to
confess everything, even if that got her husband in trouble.

She and her husband acted together. If God had intended the husband to be
the "leader of the household" with authority to command his wife's obedience,
then Ananias should have borne sole responsibility for the act. If wives have
a moral obligation to yield to their husbands, then she gave the right answer,
that is, affirming what he told her to say. Indeed, if Ananias had any leadership or authority over her whatsoever, then one would expect her guilt to
be somewhat lessened. But no, she was judged by God to be completely and
individually responsible for her actions, independent of her husband. And she
suffered the identical punishment. This account of God's judgment seems to
contradict the idea that a husband has authority over his wife.

Romans 16:
Paul Greets Seven Women Church Leaders including Deacon Phoebe and the Apostle Junia[22]

Hey, Theo, I have a pop quiz for you! Who wrote the book of Romans? What is that? You said Paul? No, you are wrong!

Don't worry, I am not starting some biblical authorship debate. Paul did author Romans, but he had some health condition, probably poor eyesight (Galatians 4:15; 6:11; 2 Thessalonians 3:17), that affected his ability to write, so he did not physically write the book of Romans. The writer of Romans is, in fact, Tertius:

> I, Tertius, who wrote down this letter, greet you in the Lord.
> (Romans 16:22)

Here we see Tertius playfully saying hello to fellow believers, after writing this letter as Paul's secretary. I only raise this bit of trivia to point out that Paul wrote with help from fellow believers, his co-laborers. And at the end of Romans, he acknowledges some of them. The first and most important person he acknowledges is Phoebe:

> I commend to you our sister Phoebe, a deacon of the church in Cenchreae. I ask you to receive her in the Lord in a way worthy of his people and to give her any help she may need from you, for she has been the benefactor of many people, including me. (Romans 16:1–2)

In the NIV, Phoebe is called a "deacon," reflecting the Greek word *diakonos*. But some versions identify Phoebe as a "servant." Throughout the New Testament, this word is translated variously as "servant," "deacon," or "minister." For example, consider the following verses (the bolded word is *diakonos*):

---

22. For further discussion, see Payne, *Man and Woman, One in Christ*, 61–68.

*He has made us competent as **ministers** of a new covenant—not of the letter but of the Spirit; for the letter kills, but the Spirit gives life.* (2 Corinthians 3:6)

*Rather, as **servants** of God we commend ourselves in every way: in great endurance; in troubles, hardships and distresses* (2 Corinthians 6:4)

*Paul and Timothy, servants of Christ Jesus, To all God's holy people in Christ Jesus at Philippi, together with the overseers and **deacons**:* (Philippians 1:1)

As expected, we must use the context to determine which definition is the right one. We are told Phoebe is "(diakonos) *of the church in Cenchreae.*" Could it mean servant? Well, when this word is translated "servant" elsewhere, Paul is referring to issues such as being a "servant of God," "servants of Christ," "servant of the gospel," "servant in the Lord," and "servants of righteousness." Nowhere else does Paul say that any church had a "servant." "Servant," therefore, does not fit here, so Phoebe was either a deacon or minister. Furthermore, we see that the Greek states, "Phoebe, who is (*ousan*) *deacon of the church in Cenchreae.*" "Who is" makes it "very much more natural . . . to understand it as referring to a definite office."[23]

Next, Paul asks the Romans *"to receive her."* He says this because he chose Phoebe to deliver his letter to the Roman churches. Therefore, she would have read it to them and would have answered any theological questions they might have asked. Note that Romans was Paul's most theologically comprehensive letter, and he entrusted its delivery and explanation to a woman.

Finally, Paul identifies Phoebe as a "benefactor." However, this is probably not the best translation. Elsewhere in the New Testament, a different word is used for "benefactor," *euergetēs*, meaning "one who does good." The word here, *prostatis*, combines the words for "in rank before" and "standing," and so he

---

23. C. E. B. Cranfield, *A Critical and Exegetical Commentary on the Epistle to the Romans* (ICC; 2 vols.; Edinburgh: T. & T. Clark, 1979) 2:781, who also adds, "'a' (or possibly 'the') deacon of the church."

emphasizes the respect she should be given. The president of a synagogue or society was called its *prostatēs*. The verb form of this noun is *proistēmi*, which means "to rule over." Every occurrence of this verb that could fit this context is about leaders. For example, its translation is bold in the following verses:

- *if it* [one's gift] *is to **lead**, do it diligently* (Romans 12:8)

- respect those . . . **who are over you** in the Lord
  (1 Thessalonians 5:12 RSV)

- *The elders **who direct the affairs of the church** are worthy of double honor* (1 Timothy 5:17)

- Church officials must **be in control** of their own families
  (1 Timothy 3:4, 5, 12 CEV)

All this gives strong confirmation that Phoebe was a leader. Paul adds that she was a leader "of many people, including me" (Romans 16:2). This implies that Paul submitted to her leadership, presumably when he was in the church in Cenchreae. Paul's description of Phoebe would have encouraged those hearing this letter to value her as a reliable resource regarding its meaning and significance.

Theo, in your church, deacons probably help manage the physical needs of the church. But Phoebe's description doesn't sound like this, does it? Therefore, Phoebe sounds much more like a minister.

In the final greetings of Romans, Paul repeatedly affirms the equality of man and woman by identifying women as laboring alongside men in ministry. In Romans 16, Paul identifies the name and Christian ministry of ten people. Seven of these ten are women! He mentions that many women "labor" or "work hard" (*kopiaō*). In addition to Phoebe, Paul identifies (in bold):

- ***Priscilla*** and *Aquila, my co-workers in Christ Jesus. They risked their lives for me. Not only I but all the churches of the Gentiles are grateful for them. Greet also the church that meets in their house.* (cf. Paul's co-workers, the women Euodia and Syntyche in Philippians 4:3) (Romans 16:3–5)

- *Mary, who worked very hard* (kopiaō) *for you.* (Romans 16:6)

- *Andronicus and **Junia**, my fellow Jews who have been in prison with me. They are outstanding among the apostles, and they were in Christ before I was.* (Romans 16:7)

- ***Tryphaena** and **Tryphosa**, those women who work hard* (kopiaō) *in the Lord.* (Romans 16:12)

- *My dear friend **Persis**, another woman who has worked very hard* (kopiaō) *in the Lord.* (Romans 16:12)

Theo, it cannot be stressed enough that Paul is listing the seven women not simply as believers but as ministry leaders. After all, he greets many believers in this passage but describes only ten as ministry leaders, and seven of those are women. The three men are Aquila, Andronicus, and Urbanus. The first two are listed with their wives, highlighting their shared authority. Paul's naming such a high proportion of women leaders indicates a level of female leadership in the early church exceptional for that culture.

The significance of those who "labor" and "work hard" in the church becomes obvious in the use of these words elsewhere in Paul's letters. Paul tells us that we are to submit ourselves to all co-laborers in Christ (without regard to gender):

> *You know that the household of Stephanas were the first converts in Achaia, and they have devoted themselves to the service of the Lord's people. I urge you, brothers and sisters, to submit to such people and to everyone who joins in the work and labors* (kopiaō) *at it.* (1 Corinthians 16:15–16)

> *Now we ask you, brothers and sisters, to acknowledge those who work hard* (kopiaō) *among you, who care for you in the Lord and who admonish you. Hold them in the highest regard because of their work.* (1 Thessalonians 5:12–13a)

1 Corinthians 7:
Equality between Husbands and Wives[24]

Before we get to the tough passages, let's start with an easy one: 1 Corinthians 7. This chapter is Paul's longest and most detailed treatment of marriage, and it is simply stunning! It affirms equal opportunities, rights, and responsibilities for wives and husbands regarding various issues related to marriage, including sexual relations, divorce, singleness, and sanctification. Throughout this chapter, Paul addresses men and women as equals—again and again balancing his wording perfectly to emphasize this equality. Regarding each issue, Paul affirms that husbands and wives have equal rights and responsibilities!

The first four issues deal with marital intimacy:

> But since sexual immorality is occurring, each man should have sexual relations with his own wife, and each woman with her own husband. (1 Corinthians 7:2)

> The husband should fulfill his marital duty to his wife, and likewise the wife to her husband. (1 Corinthians 7:3)

> The wife does not have authority over her own body but yields it to her husband. In the same way, the husband does not have authority over his own body but yields it to his wife. (1 Corinthians 7:4)

> Do not deprive each other except perhaps by mutual consent and for a time, so that you may devote yourselves to prayer. (1 Corinthians 7:5)

The next five issues deal with divorce and remarriage, including the sanctification of an unbelieving spouse:

> To the married I give this command (not I, but the Lord): A wife must not separate from her husband. But if she does, she must remain

---

24. For further discussion, see Payne, *Man and Woman, One in Christ*, 105–108.

unmarried or else be reconciled to her husband. And a husband must not divorce his wife. (1 Corinthians 7:10–11)

To the rest I say this (I, not the Lord): If any brother has a wife who is not a believer and she is willing to live with him, he must not divorce her. And if a woman has a husband who is not a believer and he is willing to live with her, she must not divorce him. (1 Corinthians 7:12–13)

For the unbelieving husband has been sanctified through his wife, and the unbelieving wife has been sanctified through her believing husband. Otherwise your children would be unclean, but as it is, they are holy. (1 Corinthians 7:14)

But if the unbeliever leaves, let it be so. The brother or sister is not bound in such circumstances; God has called us to live in peace. (1 Corinthians 7:15)

How do you know, wife, whether you will save your husband? Or, how do you know, husband, whether you will save your wife? (1 Corinthians 7:16)

The final two issues deal with motivations for men and women to get married or to stay single. For either gender, the advice is the same:

But if you do marry, you have not sinned; and if a virgin marries, she has not sinned. (1 Corinthians 7:28)

An unmarried man is concerned about the Lord's affairs—how he can please the Lord. But a married man is concerned about the affairs of this world—how he can please his wife—and his interests are divided. An unmarried woman or virgin is concerned about the Lord's affairs: Her aim is to be devoted to the Lord in both body and spirit. But a married woman is concerned about the affairs of this world—how she can please her husband. (1 Corinthians 7:32–34)

In summary, Theo, Paul is encouraging men and women to stay single, so they may be more devoted to God's work. However, Paul also blesses those who desire to get married and describes how a Christian marriage should operate. Paul here, in his longest discussion of marriage by far, does not describe any hierarchy within the marriage, nor does he give either person the final word or veto power. Rather, through perfectly balanced wording, he repeatedly emphasizes the equal rights and responsibilities of husband and wife.

1 Corinthians 8–10: The Supremacy of Christ

Before we jump into 1 Corinthians 11, Theo, I want to look at the chapters between chapter 7 (about the equal rights and responsibilities of wives and husbands) and chapter 11.

In each of these three chapters, Paul is talking about our freedom in Christ. Although we do have great freedom in Christ, we are also slaves to Christ. Our responsibility to our brothers and sisters, and to spreading the gospel, is more important than our freedoms. Key verses from these chapters teach this:

> *Be careful, however, that the exercise of your rights does not become a stumbling block to the weak.* (1 Corinthians 8:9)

> *Though I am free and belong to no one, I have made myself a slave to everyone, to win as many as possible. To the Jews I became like a Jew, to win the Jews. To those under the law I became like one under the law (though I myself am not under the law), so as to win those under the law. To those not having the law I became like one not having the law (though I am not free from God's law but am under Christ's law), so as to win those not having the law. To the weak I became weak, to win the weak. I have become all things to all people so that by all possible means I might save some. I do all this for the sake of the gospel, that I may share in its blessings.* (1 Corinthians 9:19–23)

> *So whether you eat or drink or whatever you do, do it all for the glory of God. Do not cause anyone to stumble, whether Jews, Greeks or the church of God—even as I try to please everyone in every way. For I am not seeking my own good but the good of many, so that they may be saved.* (1 Corinthians 10:31–33)

Above all, Christ must reign supreme in our lives. Our primary focus must be on him and spreading his gospel. We should do everything we can to support this mission. With that in mind, let's consider 1 Corinthians 11.

.

1 Corinthians 11:
Head Coverings for Men and Women[25]

We have now arrived at the chapter of the Bible which is single-handedly responsible for Christian women all over the world wearing some sort of cloth on their head and Christian men not wearing a cloth on their head. It is widely assumed that this passage reinforces a universal church custom that women must wear a garment over their heads in Christian worship. But does this interpretation fit Paul's wording or cultural context? We just read how Paul desires that he (and by extension, we) should strive to be all things to all people for the sake of the gospel. Doesn't it seem strange that in this context Paul would insist that some of us wear a piece of cloth over our head? Do we really think Paul was saying, "Whatever you do, do it all for the glory of God, but make sure you have the proper head covering"? That doesn't make any sense. How do such rules advance the gospel?

INTRODUCTION

Maybe Paul is simply enforcing an existing biblical mandate? But nowhere in the Bible is there any comparable head-covering prohibition for men or requirement for women.

Could Paul be enforcing a social norm of the time? Corinth had been a Greek city until 146 BC, and then a Roman city after 46 BC. Maybe women in Corinth were just expected to wear head coverings. But since Corinth was a big city with a diverse population, it would not have had a single social norm. And if we search for sculptures illustrating first-century Greco-Roman women, we find many examples like these:

Portrait Bust of a Woman,
140 CE–150 CE,
The Art Institute of Chicago

25. For further discussion, see Payne, *Man and Woman, One in Christ*, 109.

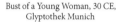

| Bust of a Young Woman, 30 CE, Glyptothek Munich | Marble Portrait Bust of a Woman, 100 CE–120 CE, Metropolitan Museum of Art | Marble Portrait of a Young Woman, 150 CE–175 CE, Metropolitan Museum of Art |

While one can find some sculptures showing women with a head covering, most do not, and certainly not enough to demonstrate any kind of a social norm requiring head coverings.

Furthermore, several writers from that time period and many current historians agree that head coverings were simply not the norm.[26]

Finally, while there is no consensus that the Bible gives head-covering garment rules, the Bible clearly forbids elaborate hairstyles, including:

> *I also want the women to dress modestly, with decency and propriety, adorning themselves, not with elaborate hairstyles or*[27] *gold or pearls or expensive clothes . . .* (1 Timothy 2:9)

> *Your beauty should not come from outward adornment, such as elaborate hairstyles and the wearing of gold jewelry or fine clothes.* (1 Peter 3:3)

---

26. Payne, *Man and Woman, One in Christ*, 152–162.
27. In Greek, both in 1 Timothy 2:9 and 1 Peter 3:3, this conjunction is "and", unlike the following "or" conjunctions. Both Paul and Peter, therefore, prohibit elaborate, wealth-flaunting hairstyles that *combine* braids with gold. Neither Paul nor Peter prohibits the common wearing of braids or gold in isolation, such as the modern custom of wearing a gold wedding ring. There were no cultured pearls then, so pearls and expensive clothing also flaunted wealth.

But if all women's hair were covered up with a garment, they wouldn't need these rules about specific hairstyles, because no such hairstyle would be visible.

Nowhere else in the Bible is there any mandate that corresponds to the usual interpretation of 1 Corinthians 11:2–16 as regarding head-covering garments. In fact, the verses just cited above seem to assume that women's hair is visible. Furthermore, there was no clearly documented social norm at that time and in that culture that forbade men from covering their heads or required women to cover their heads. So then, the question we must ask ourselves is, **"Why does Paul all of a sudden decide to make strict regulations regarding head-covering garments?!"**

Here is the answer: He does not! This passage is not about head-covering garments. There is no word in this chapter that demands a "head covering" in the sense of a garment covering the head. And with that bit of introduction, we can begin.

1 CORINTHIANS 11:3: WHAT DOES "HEAD" CONVEY?[28]

> *But I want you to realize that the head of every man is Christ, and the head of the woman is man, and the head of Christ is God.*
> (1 Corinthians 11:3)

This chapter certainly does not lack for controversy. In this verse, the key question that has been debated at length is "What does 'head' mean?" The Greek word used here is *kephalē*, which simply means "head" (that thing on top of your shoulders). The primary two competing explanations of the meaning of "head" here are "authority," as in the head of the company, or "source," as in the head of the river. Many books and articles have been written on this topic, but I will simply give a few reasons why the second definition makes the most sense here:

- Paul is not describing a hierarchy. If "head" meant authority, then the natural way to express the authority would be either a top-down or bottom-up hierarchy (e.g., God is the authority over Christ, Christ is

---

28. For further discussion, see Payne, *Man and Woman, One in Christ*, 113–139.

the authority over man, and man is the authority over woman). But nothing in Paul's word order fits a hierarchy.

- The order given, however, does match up with the historical sequence of these source relations.

  ○ First, man came from Christ (1 Corinthians 8:6 "*Jesus Christ, through whom all things came*"; 1 Corinthians 11:7 refers to this event, man created in the image of God).

  ○ Then woman came from man (created from man's rib)— 1 Corinthians 1:8 and 12 explicitly state this.

  ○ Finally, to provide redemption, Christ came from the Godhead in the incarnation.

- The only reference to authority in this chapter is an affirmation of the woman's authority over her head in verse 10. Other than that one verse, authority is not discussed at all. But as we will see in 1 Corinthians 11:7, 8, and 12, this section does deal with origins and who came from whom.

- If you take "authority" as the definition of "head," then Paul would be saying that God is the authority over the risen Christ. But nowhere does the Bible teach a hierarchy of authority within the eternal persons of the Trinity. In fact, early church councils affirmed that the persons of the Trinity are equal in being, power, and glory and called the eternal subordination of the Son to the Father heresy.[29]

- In other letters, when Paul describes Christ as the head of the church, he is describing how Christ is the source of the church or the source of the body's growth, as in:

  Instead, speaking the truth in love, we will grow to become in every respect the mature body of him who is the head, that is, Christ. From him the whole body, joined and held together by every supporting ligament, grows and builds itself up in love, as each part does its work. (Ephesians 4:15–16)

---

29. For further discussion, see Kevin Giles, *Jesus and the Father: Modern Evangelicals Reinvent the Doctrine of the Trinity* (Grand Rapids, MI: Zondervan, 2006).

They have lost connection with the head, from whom the whole body, supported and held together by its ligaments and sinews, grows as God causes it to grow. (Colossians 2:19)

- In Colossians 1:18, it says, "*And he is the head of the body, the church, who is the beginning* (archē)" (archē in this context refers to Christ as the "source" of the church, not the "beginning" of the church.).[30]

- Many church fathers explain that all three occurrences of "head" in 1 Corinthians 11:3 mean "source." For example, Cyril of Alexandria (died AD 444): "Luke [3:38, 'Adam from God'] … explains the source of man, the Creator God. Thus we say that 'the head (*kephalē*) of every man is Christ,' for man was made through him and brought into existence … 'And the head (*kephalē*) of woman is the man,' because she was taken out of his flesh and so indeed has him as her source. Similarly, 'the head (*kephalē*) of Christ is God,' because He is from Him according to nature: for the Word was begotten out of God the Father."[31]

- Of the 180 instances where the Hebrew Scriptures' word for "head" means "leader," the standard Greek Old Testament only once translates it *kephalē* clearly as a metaphor for "leader."[32] This shows how foreign to Greek it was to use *kephalē* to convey "authority."

- Dictionaries of classical secular Greek since the twelfth century commonly list *kephalē* ("head") meaning "source" but cite no pre-New-Testament examples meaning "authority."

---

30. The earliest manuscripts' detailed apposition: "he is the head … who is the source" (*autos estin hē kephalē … hos estin hē archē*) explains that "head" means "the source of the body's life" (TEV) or "origin" (NEB). They have no punctuation separating "he is the head" from "who is the source." The immediately following "the firstborn from the dead" and verse 20's "by making peace through his blood, shed on the cross" identify how Christ became the source of the body's life and so further support this meaning.
31. *de recta fide ad Arcadiam et Marinam* 1.1.5.5(2).63.
32. Philip B. Payne, "What About Headship? From Hierarchy to Equality" in Mutual by Design: A Better Model of Christian Marriage (ed. Elizabeth Beyer; Minneapolis, MN: CBE International, 2017) 141–160, 226–232 argues that all other alleged LXX instances were added by Origen, are explained in context to mean something other than "leader," or state eis kephalēn, which readers probably understood as a simile, "as head," not a metaphor "is head."

1 CORINTHIANS 11:4:
WHAT IS THE DISHONOR OF A MAN COVERING HIS HEAD?[33]

Okay, Theo, it's time to examine what Paul says about head coverings!

> *Every man who prays or prophesies with his head covered dishonors his head.* (1 Corinthians 11:4)

First off, notice that Paul is using a bit of word play here by using two definitions of "head" in the same sentence. The first "head" refers to the man's physical head (the thing on top of his shoulders); the second "head" refers to Christ as the man's "head,"[34] as stated in 11:3. The verse is saying that the man dishonors Christ by having his head covered.

Okay, that seems to be very straightforward, doesn't it? If you are a man, then doing religious things while covering your head is bad! Except, it's not that simple. Consider how Aaron was dressed in the Old Testament:

> ***Put the turban on his head*** *and attach the sacred emblem to the turban. Take the anointing oil and anoint him by pouring it on his head. Bring his sons and dress them in tunics **and fasten caps on them**. Then tie sashes on Aaron and his sons. The priesthood is theirs by a lasting ordinance. Then you shall ordain Aaron and his sons.* (Exodus 29:6–9)

Got that? Aaron was wearing a holy turban on his head, and his sons were wearing holy caps. And this was not just a fluke. It's mentioned again multiple times, as in Leviticus:

> *This is how Aaron is to enter the Most Holy Place: . . . he is to tie the linen sash around him and **put on the linen turban**. These are sacred garments; so he must bathe himself with water before he puts them on.* (Leviticus 16:3–4)

---

33. For further discussion, see Payne, *Man and Woman, One in Christ*, 141–146.
34. "Head" here probably also indicates the shame one causes to oneself, which was another metaphorical meaning for "head."

In the Old Testament, priests were commanded to wear a garment over their heads. That head covering was sacred. This was pious, not disgraceful.

So, Theo, are you confused now? The Old Testament seems ultra-clear that priests were supposed to have a covering on their heads, especially when performing religious duties. But now it looks like Paul is saying the opposite. Maybe Paul is saying that men should not wear anything on their head because that makes them look like an Old Testament priest, and we no longer have priests? But Paul doesn't say that, and besides, that sounds like a weird rule. Or maybe it's just that our understanding of 1 Corinthians 11:4 is wrong? Possibly . . . and if we grab an interlinear Greek Bible, we see that, yes, indeed, the translation is wrong. The phrase that the NIV translates *"with his head covered"* in Greek says "having down from the head." So, the verse literally reads, "Every man who prays or prophesies having down from the head dishonors his head."

This sounds a bit wonky, however, and leaves us wondering what it means (which explains why the translators changed it to make the passage sound more natural). What is this thing Paul is talking about? What is something that is "down from the head"? The answer that best fits the context is—hair! If you glance a few verses ahead, you will note several references to hair, which I will be discussing in the next few sections.

Paul is talking about hair, not head-covering garments. And specifically, having hair that hangs down long. It was not wrong for men to wear head coverings. In fact, it was customary for leaders in Roman worship (Corinth was a Roman city at this time) to drape a garment over their heads, the *"capite velato"* custom. This was not disgraceful, but a sign of piety. So then, Paul was not opposing men wearing something on their heads. He was opposing men leading worship with long hair hanging down. Why? Paul does not tell us his reasons right away, but he will get to them in a few verses.

For now, understand that 1 Corinthians 11:4 addresses the shame a man brought on himself and on Christ his creator-source when praying and prophesying with long hair hanging down.

1 Corinthians 11:5–6:
What Is the Dishonor of a Woman Uncovering Her Head?[35]

> *But every woman who prays or prophesies with her head uncovered dishonors her head—it is the same as having her head shaved. For if a woman does not cover her head, she might as well have her hair cut off; but if it is a disgrace for a woman to have her hair cut off or her head shaved, then she should cover her head.* (1 Corinthians 11:5–6)

Before I talk about head coverings, Theo, you should note that the first part of this verse assumes that women are praying and prophesying in their gatherings, just like the men were doing. And those were the most important parts of the service. New Testament churches were small groups meeting at someone's home—there was not a sermon afterward done by the senior pastor. Men and women were participating equally in the life of New Testament churches.

Here again Paul is using the same bit of word play as before. The first "head" refers to the woman's physical head. The second "head" refers to the woman's "head" (source), which 11:3 explains is man. The verse is saying that the woman dishonors man by not covering her head. But what does Paul mean by this?

The Greek phrase that is translated "with her head uncovered" (*akatakalyptō tē kephalē*) is simply "with uncovered head." You may be saying, "Aha! It must be talking about head-covering garments!" But what does removing a head-covering garment have to do with shaving one's head? These things have no obvious connection. It would be very helpful if we found another biblical passage that dealt with uncovering a woman's head to help us understand this passage.

The good news is that there is such a passage! Numbers 5 deals with the situation when a man's wife is suspected of adultery, without a witness to the act. In this case, the woman is supposed to be subject to the "bitter water" test to prove her guilt or innocence. The test begins by "uncovering" the woman's head (as seen here in the KJV):

---

35. For further discussion, see Payne, *Man and Woman, One in Christ*, 147–173.

And the priest shall set the woman before the LORD, and uncover the woman's head, and put the offering of memorial in her hands, which is the jealousy offering: and the priest shall have in his hand the bitter water that causeth the curse: (Numbers 5:18 KJV)

The Greek Old Testament uses words similar to Paul's: *apokalypsei tēn kephalēn tēs gynaikos,* "uncover the head of the woman." However, virtually all recent Bible translations correctly reflect the Hebrew original and show that this does not mean the priest is removing something from her head. Rather, it refers to letting her hair down, as seen, for example, in the NIV:

After the priest has had the woman stand before the LORD, he shall loosen her hair and place in her hands the reminder-offering, the grain offering for jealousy, while he himself holds the bitter water that brings a curse. (Numbers 5:18)

A similar verse is Leviticus 13:45, which uses the same Greek word Paul uses in 1 Corinthians 11:5 (*akatakalyptos*) and the same Hebrew word as Numbers 5:18 to describe an "uncovered head." Some Bible versions translate this verse as:

As for the leper who has the infection, his clothes shall be torn, and the hair of his head shall be uncovered, and he shall cover his mustache and cry, 'Unclean! Unclean!' (Leviticus 13:45 NASB 1977)

However, virtually all recent Bible translations agree that nothing is being removed from the leper's head. Rather, their hair is simply let loose:[36]

Anyone with such a defiling disease must wear torn clothes, let their hair be unkempt, cover the lower part of their face and cry out, 'Unclean! Unclean!' (Leviticus 13:45)

---

36. The standard Hebrew dictionary (HALOT 3:970) explains this verb's meaning "with ראשׁ ['head'] . . . Lv 10₆ 13₄₅ 21₁₀ . . . to let down the hair . . . Nu 5₁₈." This is only occurrence in the Greek Old Testament of "uncovered," *akatakalyptos*.

These two passages confirm our answer: "uncovering a woman's head" refers to "loosening her hair" or "letting her hair down." Consequently, when her hair is put up, her head is "covered." This understanding is further confirmed in verse 15: "long hair is given to her as a covering." Covering your head with your long hair means putting your hair up over your head.

But why does it dishonor a man if a woman lets her hair down when praying or prophesying in church? When a woman's hair was let down loose, it symbolized undisciplined sexuality.[37] The reason Paul opposed women leading in worship with their hair let down was that in so doing they were symbolizing their sexual availability, putting on themselves the accusation of adultery. And in Paul's day, if a woman was convicted of adultery, her hair was cut off. This explains why all the women in the sculptures I showed you earlier had their long hair put up. To let their hair down would have symbolized undisciplined sexuality and would have shamed both themselves and their husbands.

This also explains why 1 Corinthians 11:5 says that a woman who uncovers her hair by letting it down is "one and the same as the shorn woman." Paul wants such a woman to appreciate the shame she is causing to herself and to her husband by letting her hair down loose. If she is going to put on herself the symbol of an accused adulteress by letting her long hair down, then she should accept the shame of the punishment of adultery by going ahead and cutting off her hair. However, Paul would prefer the woman to simply cover her head, not with a garment, but with her long hair. This is confirmed in verse 15, which I will get to soon.

Why would women let their hair down to prophesy in the church in Corinth? Dionysiac revelries[38] were infamous for women (called "maenads") letting their hair down, ecstatic "prophesying," and engaging in orgies. Pervasive Dionysiac influence in Corinth, with its strong emphasis on freedom from cultural restraints, best explains why at least one woman in the Corinthian

37. C. R. Hallpike, "Social Hair", *Man* NS 4 (1969) 256–264.
38. Dionysus was the god of wine. The rampant illicit sex in its revelries in the hills near Corinth caused the cult to be banned in Rome.

church, perhaps wanting to express her freedom in Christ, let her hair down when praying or prophesying. It is novel, probably Dionysiac-inspired, Corinthian offenses that Paul prohibits.

1 CORINTHIANS 11:7–9:
WHY A MAN OUGHT NOT COVER HIS HEAD[39]

> *A man ought not to cover his head, since he is the image and glory of God; but woman is the glory of man. For man did not come from woman, but woman from man; neither was man created for woman, but woman for man.* (1 Corinthians 11:7–9)

Wow, another doozy of a passage! Theo, as I'm sure you can imagine, these verses have been horribly misinterpreted and misapplied to women for thousands of years, implying that women are not created in the image of God, but rather in the image of man, and that women were created just to serve men.

This passage may seem difficult to understand at first, but if we use the same context as the previous verses, its meaning is straightforward. So far, Paul has told us that:

- Men should not pray or prophecy with long hair hanging down.

- Women should not pray or prophecy with long hair hanging down, either.

- Women should put their hair up while praying or prophesying, to cover their head.

There is then one missing case: "Is it okay for men with long hair to put their hair up, thereby covering their head?" Paul discusses that case in these verses and concludes that a man with long hair should not cover his head with long hair like women do. If a man with long hair should not let it hang down, and he should not put it up, then he should not have long hair at all—and Paul makes that exact point in a few verses, reflecting the common Hellenistic

---

39. For further discussion, see Payne, *Man and Woman, One in Christ*, 175–181.

convention of his day that men should not have long hair. Here he gives his reasons why men should not cover their heads with effeminate hairstyles:

- **The man is the image and glory of God.** First, the NIV's addition of the word "the" before "image" can give the false impression that man is the single image and glory of God (and therefore, women are not). But there is no "the" in the Greek. Man is not the only image-bearer of God. We know from Genesis that God made both man and woman in God's image. Recall that "*God created mankind in his own image, in the image of God he created them; male and female he created them*" (Genesis 1:27).

  Paul is saying that man was created in God's image, displaying the glory of God's creativity. God delights in his creation. And man should trust God's design for sexuality, which is . . .

- **Woman is the glory of man.** Paul's point is that it is a woman—not another man—that is the glory of man. The word "glory" means something along the lines of pride and joy or delight. God created woman to be man's sexual mate. Literature contemporary to Paul condemns men wearing effeminate hairstyles because this was associated with men attracting homosexual hookups. Dionysus, the god of wine, is often depicted effeminately. Dionysiac revelry was infamous for homosexual hookups (a concern of Paul in 1 Corinthians 6:9–11).

  Most translations begin this phrase with the conjunction "but," which indicates a contrasting phrase. However, the word here (*de*) is probably best translated as "and" because it introduces a second reason men should not do this. It is not the Greek word *alla* that specifically means "but." The phrase that contrasts with "*A man ought not to cover his head*" comes in 11:10 regarding what "*a woman ought to*" do with "*her head*," namely cover it.

- **For man did not come from woman, but woman from man; neither was man created for the woman, but woman for the man.** Paul is not denigrating women. Paul is reminding us of the creation of the first woman from one of Adam's ribs, and specifically that woman was created for man, to be man's mate, his glory, his intimate

partner. Effeminate display of hair depicted a man presenting himself as a sexual mate for other men.[40]

Paul is saying that men should not lead worship with long hair because in that
culture, they were inviting homosexual hookups.

1 CORINTHIANS 11:10:
WHY A WOMAN OUGHT TO EXERCISE AUTHORITY OVER HER HEAD[41]

The previous three verses described what a man "ought to" do. Now, Paul tells
us what a woman "ought to" do.

> *It is for this reason that a woman ought to have authority over her*
> *own head, because of the angels.* (1 Corinthians 11:10)

Three parts of this verse have often been misunderstood:

1. *for this reason*—(what reason?)

2. *ought to have authority over her own head*—(huh?)

3. *because of the angels*—(why does Paul bring up angels?)

We will consider them in order:

For this reason: This phrase can be translated "therefore" because every other
time Paul uses the combination of "for this reason (*dia touto*) . . . because of
(*dia*) . . . ," he uses *dia touto* to apply the reasons just stated to what follows.[42]
In verses 7–9, Paul had just given several reasons why men leading in worship
should not display effeminate hair. Each is also a good reason for a woman to
put up her long hair:

• Man *is the image and glory of God*, so his wife should not dishonor
  him by letting her hair down in public.

---

40. For further discussion, see Philip B. Payne, "Wild Hair and Gender Equality in
    1 Corinthians 11:2–16", *Priscilla Papers* 20, 1 (2006) 9–18.
41. For further discussion, see Payne, *Man and Woman, One in Christ*, 181–187.
42. The other two "*dia touto . . . dia*" are 2 Timothy 2:8–10 and 1 Thessalonians 3:6–7.

- *Woman is the glory of man,* so she should bring glory to her husband, not shame.

- Woman was made *from man,* so she should respect her source, not humiliate him.

- Woman was made *for man,* to fulfill him, not to shame him.

Ought to have authority over her own head: This has at times been unjustifiably altered. Many older translations, including the 1984 NIV, even drastically change this verse to talk about a symbol or sign of authority:

> For this reason, and because of the angels, the woman ought to have a sign of authority on her head. (1 Corinthians 11:10 NIV 1984)

But there is nothing in this verse that can possibly be translated as "symbol" or "sign."

So, what does this phrase mean? The first word, "ought," indicates a moral imperative. We can deduce the specific meaning of "have authority" in this verse by simply observing Paul's similar usage of the same phrase earlier in 1 Corinthians:

> *But the man who has settled the matter in his own mind, who is under no compulsion* **but has control over** *his own will, and who has made up his mind not to marry the virgin—this man also does the right thing.* (1 Corinthians 7:37)

That phrase, "has control over (*exousian echei*) his own will," translates the same Greek words as "have authority (*exousian echein*)" in 11:10. Both refer to exercising control over something. So, the phrase "ought to have authority over her own head" simply means to "have control of" or "exercise control over" her own head. In other words, Paul is just saying that the woman should exercise control over her head by putting her hair up on her head to avoid symbolizing undisciplined sexuality.

Because of the angels: The context here is worship, and Paul refers to angels in the context of worship elsewhere:

> *We have been made a spectacle to the whole universe, to angels as well as to human beings.* (1 Corinthians 4:9)

> *I charge you, in the sight of God and Christ Jesus and the elect angels . . .* (1 Timothy 5:21)

This fits the New Testament theme that Christian worship reflects the presence of angels before the throne of God (Matthew 18:10). If the symbolism of undisciplined sexuality and the shame it causes both you and your husband are not sufficient reason, "because of the angels" (who observe worship and report directly to God) gives one more reason why women should exercise control over their heads by not letting their hair hang loose.

1 CORINTHIANS 11:11–12: MAN AND WOMAN ARE NOT SEPARATE IN THE LORD[43]

> *Nevertheless, in the Lord woman is not independent of man, nor is man independent of woman. For as woman came from man, so also man is born of woman. But everything comes from God.* (1 Corinthians 11:11–12)

Because verse 10 is about woman's obligation to exercise her own authority, verse 11 begins, "Nevertheless, woman is not . . ." If Paul had intended verse 10 to affirm man's authority, he would have begun verse 11, "Nevertheless, man is not . . ." as some versions change it to read! Verse 11 teaches, instead, that "woman is not separate from man, nor is man separate from woman in the Lord."

Paul begins verse 11 with the word "nevertheless." Paul consistently uses this word to cut off the discussion and emphasize what is important. Although Paul has just given different instructions for men and women, he makes it clear that the more important principle is that in Christ, men and women are

---

43. For further discussion, see Payne, *Man and Woman, One in Christ*, 189–198.

"not separate" from each other. *"In the Lord"* specifies that Paul is now talking about believers' standing in Christ.

"Independent" is not the most accurate translation here—most Greek dictionaries do not even list "independent" regarding persons as one of its meanings. Rather, they give the meaning "separate" or "set apart." Paul affirms here that in the Lord, men and women are not set apart from each other but are equal—both have equal standing and equal rights. This is why women may pray and prophesy in church!

Theo, remember back in Genesis 2, when I discussed whether the fact that man was created before woman indicates that man has some sort of authority or special leadership role over woman? Well, here is your answer! In reference specifically to creation,[44] verse 12 says that just as woman came from man, now every man is born through woman. Both owe respect to the other as their source. And all this comes from the Godhead! Paul affirms that "woman is not separate from man, and man is not separate from woman" in the context of men and women leading worship in prayer and prophecy. Therefore, there should be no separation between man and woman when it comes to leadership in worship.

---

44. Verse 12's phrase, "from man (*ek tou andros*)," is identical to the Greek of Genesis 2:23: "she was taken from the man (*ek tou andros*)" and so refers to creation.

1 Corinthians 11:13–16: Final Word on Long Hair[45]

Judge for yourselves: Is it proper for a woman to pray to God with her head uncovered? Does not the very nature of things teach you that if a man has long hair, it is a disgrace to him, but that if a woman has long hair, it is her glory? For long hair is given to her as a covering. If anyone wants to be contentious about this, we have no other practice—nor do the churches of God. (1 Corinthians 11:13–16)

In Paul's concluding remarks, he says *it is a disgrace* for a man to have long hair. Literature contemporary to Paul confirms this repeatedly. A woman's long hair, however, is her glory if she uses it as a covering, as literature and art contemporary to Paul also confirm. Nobody should be contentious about this in church.

These last few verses should remove any doubt that hair is the covering Paul is talking about.

Here for the first and only time in this paragraph, Paul uses the word for a head-covering garment, not to require one, but to assert that a woman's hair has been given to her to serve as a head covering. Therefore, when a woman's hair is put up modestly over her head, her head is covered. A woman does not need to put a garment over her head to "cover" it.

Paul reiterates the focus of his concern—women properly praying and prophesying in church.

The NIV translation of the last clause, *"we have no other practice—nor do the churches of God,"* is not accurate. The word translated as *"other"* means the exact opposite and should be translated "we have no such practice," as Greek dictionaries make clear. In this case, the KJV is correct:

we have no such custom . . . (1 Corinthians 11:16 KJV)

---

45. For further discussion, see Payne, *Man and Woman, One in Christ*, 199–215.

Paul uses the conjunction *oude* to join "we" and "the churches or God." He typically uses *oude* to join two elements to convey a single idea (I will discuss this more in the section on Galatians 3:28). Paul is not distinguishing himself from the churches but identifying with them as he always does elsewhere, so this should be translated: "We, the churches of God, have no such custom." This clarifies that these hairstyles undermining Christian morality were not the custom in any other churches.

Paul states that men wearing long effeminate hair and women letting their hair down was shameful. Many statements in the literature of Paul's day confirm both were shameful. Today, however, men wearing long hair is not generally regarded as shameful, effeminate, or promiscuous, nor is a woman's hair draped over her shoulders regarded as shameful. It no longer symbolizes unrestrained sexuality. If Paul were writing today, he would not prohibit either, nor should we.

Finally, as we close out this passage and get ready to move on to the next one, I am left with a strong sense of, "Sorry, what was the question again?!" I thought we were supposed to be talking about the roles of women in the church and family, and instead, we have been spending the past many sections discussing hairstyles. The reason we have considered this passage in detail is because this passage on hair lengths has been used for most of Christian history to claim that:

- Men have authority over women.

- Women need to have men in authority over them.

- Women must wear a garment on their head as a sign/symbol of man's authority over them.

- Women were created to serve men.

- Women were not created in the image of God. Rather they were created in the image of man.

- Jesus is eternally subject to God the Father, even in heaven.

Theo, do you believe any of these claims? They have all been justified by misunderstandings and bad translations of this passage. Do you remember asking me about the "slippery slope" of giving equal authority or leadership to women? Surely you can appreciate some of the consequences from the church denying equal authority and leadership to women and giving men such power over women for most of Christian history. Just consider all the injustices and abuse women have endured because of men believing that they have power over women. This has been the "slippery slope" (more like a "cliff") of not giving equal authority and leadership to women.

1 Corinthians 12: Spiritual Gifts[46]

The very next chapter repeatedly asserts that God gives spiritual gifts to all believers:

> *Now to each one the manifestation of the Spirit is given for the common good. To one there is given through the Spirit a message of wisdom, to another a message of knowledge by means of the same Spirit, to another faith by the same Spirit, to another gifts of healing by that one Spirit, to another miraculous powers, to another prophecy, to another distinguishing between spirits, to another speaking in different kinds of tongues, and to still another the interpretation of tongues. All these are the work of one and the same Spirit, and he distributes them to each one, just as he determines.* (1 Corinthians 12:7–11)

Notice that the text makes no distinction between men and women—gifts are given as the Spirit decides to distribute them. However, today nobody disputes that women are gifted, but they do dispute how women can use their gifts. And in many churches, the most controversial gift is that of teaching. So, we will skip down a bit to the discussion about the gift of teaching:

> *Now you are the body of Christ, and each one of you is a part of it. And God has placed in the church first of all apostles, second prophets, third teachers, then miracles, then gifts of healing, of helping, of guidance, and of different kinds of tongues. Are all apostles? Are all prophets? Are all teachers? Do all work miracles? Do all have gifts of healing? Do all speak in tongues? Do all interpret? Now eagerly desire the greater gifts.* (1 Corinthians 12:27–31)

---

46. For further discussion, see Payne, *Man and Woman, One in Christ*, 73, 223, 328.

In most passages about spiritual gifts, Paul lists the gifts with no order of importance. However, here he does rank the following gifts in this order of importance:

1. apostles

2. prophets

3. teachers

4. miracle workers

5. healers, helpers, guides, speakers of tongues

Paul's "*Now eagerly desire the greater gifts*" addresses the entire church, women as well as men. Would Paul command women to desire to become teachers if they were forbidden to teach? We know that Junia was a female apostle (Romans 16:7). We know that there were female prophets because Anna was one (Luke 2:36). "Philip the evangelist . . . had four unmarried daughters who prophesied" (Acts 21:8–9), and the previous chapter gives instructions for "every woman who prophesies" (11:5). We know that there were female teachers because Priscilla was one (Acts 18:26) as were Timothy's mother and grandmother (2 Timothy 1:5; 3:14–15). Since the New Testament gives examples of women in the top three categories, any interpretation that prohibits all women from teaching can't be right. It makes sense that women would be found in all "lesser" gifts as well, wouldn't it? As before, Paul gives no indication whatsoever that women are excluded from any gift.

1 Corinthians 14:34–35: Did Paul write, "Women Must Be Silent in the Churches"?[47]

Okay, it is time to tackle another doozy of a passage! Here we go.

> *Women should remain silent in the churches. They are not allowed to speak, but must be in submission, as the law says. If they want to inquire about something, they should ask their own husbands at home; for it is disgraceful for a woman to speak in the church.* (1 Corinthians 14:34–35)

Well, Theo, this passage is as simple as it is controversial. Yes, it commands women in the churches not to speak but to be silent. If you grab your Greek dictionary and look up the words, their meaning is clear and the words mean exactly what they appear to mean. The passage repeats this command with three different wordings, each clear, simple, and with no qualification. These verses have puzzled virtually everyone who has studied them, including early church theologians, for many reasons.[48]

To name just a few, first, the plain meaning of these verses contradicts many statements throughout 1 Corinthians that *all* may teach and prophesy, including verses shortly before and after 14:34–35:

- *But every woman who prays or prophesies . . .* (1 Corinthians 1:5)

- *I would like **every one of you** . . . to prophesy* (1 Corinthians 14:5)

- *While **everyone** is prophesying . . . by **all** . . .* ("all" twice in Greek 1 Corinthians 14:24)

---

47. For further discussion, see Payne, *Man and Woman, One in Christ*, 217–267.
48. Payne, *Man and Woman, One in Christ*, 227–253 lists seven reasons based on manuscript evidence and 253–265 lists nine reasons based on the content and context of these verses. You can also download free Payne's articles at www.pbpayne.com (under Publications: Articles) that identify evidence from Codex Fuldensis and Manuscript 88 that 14:34–35 was not by Paul.

- *What shall we say, brothers and sisters? When you come together, **each of you** has a hymn, or a word of instruction, a revelation, a tongue or an interpretation.* (1 Corinthians 14:26)

- *For you can **all** prophesy in turn so that everyone may be instructed and encouraged.* (1 Corinthians 14:31)

- *Therefore, my brothers and sisters, be eager to prophesy, and do not forbid speaking in tongues.* (1 Corinthians 14:39)

Second, verse 34 not only forbids women from speaking, it also demands their subjection, "as the law says (*lalein*)." This is doubly problematic. No Old Testament law forbids women from doing either one. Nor does it fit Paul's style. He almost always uses "it is written"[49] to refer to specific scriptures. The only two times he uses "as the law says" to refer to a specific law, he uses a different verb (*legō*) and quotes that law, *"You shall not covet"* (Romans 7:7) and *"it is written in the Law of Moses"* (1 Corinthians 9:8–10). Furthermore, no other passage in Paul's letters cites the law to establish a rule for Christian worship. Indeed, this seems to contradict Paul's major theme that believers are not under the law.[50]

Finally, 1 Corinthians is a letter directed to the church in Corinth. All its other commands address that church. But verse 34 directs a command to "women in the churches," which, since it immediately follows "all the churches of the saints," clearly refers to women in all the churches. A command for all women in all churches is glaringly out of place in Paul's letter addressed specifically to the church in Corinth.

So, how should we understand this passage? As I mentioned in my earlier section on "Keeping it 'Simple,'" many churches pretty much ignore it. Other churches come up with highly creative resolutions to get around this passage and allow the inclusion of women in worship, but many of these resolutions are not biblical. For example, no Bible verse says women can speak in church only

---

49. Romans 1:17; 2:24; 3:4, 10; 4:17, 23; 8:36; 9:13, 33; 10:5, 15; 11:8, 26; 12:19; 14:11; 15:3, 4, 9, 21; 1 Corinthians 1:19, 31; 2:9; 3:19; 4:6; 9:9, 10; 10:7, 11; 14:21; 15:45, 54; 2 Corinthians 4:13; 8:15; 9:9; Galatians 3:10, 13; 4:22, 27.
50. Romans 7:4–6; 10:4; 16:14–15; 1 Corinthians 9:20–21; Galatians 2:19; 3:13, 23–25; 5:18; Ephesians 2:15.

if they do not stand too close to the pulpit. Other popular resolutions include limiting the demand in 1 Corinthians 14:34–35 for silence only to disruptive chatter or judging prophecies (which is separated from 14:34–35 by four topics). These resolutions must not be correct because they permit speech in church that 14:35 prohibits, namely asking questions in church out of a desire to learn. No, this passage does not allow such trickery—it is as brutally clear as it seems.

Some scholars have argued recently that 1 Corinthians 14:34–35 expresses the view of a group in Corinth who opposed Paul and that 14:36–38 refutes it.[51] But none of the church fathers give any indication that 34–35 is a quotation, nor are verses 34–35 introduced as a false prophecy. None of the other Corinthian quotations Paul refutes are nearly this long, and verses 36–38 do not refute anything stated in 34–35.

Theo, I am afraid that the answer is that this passage does not belong. It was not part of Paul's original letter but was added later. Considering the ingrained Greek belief that women should be silent in public congregations, it is not surprising that a reader, not wanting to include women in Paul's encouragement for "all" to prophesy and teach throughout this chapter, sometime before 200 AD added in the margin the "conventional wisdom" expressed in 14:34–35, that women should be silent.

I can hear you screaming "FOUL!" and I don't blame you. And I do not take it lightly. For years I tried to defend other solutions, only to realize that no Greek reader of Paul's day would have read it according to my attempted solutions. When I finally examined the early manuscripts, I discovered crucial evidence shows that it was added at a later date.

God has faithfully preserved his Word throughout the ages, but not in a single book stored in a single location. Rather, there are many, many old manuscripts of the books of the Bible. All evangelical scholars know that throughout time, various blocks of text have been added to New Testament manuscripts. You have probably seen notes in your Bible such as the NIV at Matthew 18:11,

---

51. See Philip B. Payne, "Is 1 Corinthians 14:34–35 a Marginal Comment or a quotation? A Response to Kirk MacGregor", *Priscilla Papers* 33, 2 (Spring 2019) 24–30.

"Some manuscripts include here the words of Luke 19:10," and at John 7:53, "The earliest manuscripts . . . do not have John 7:53–8:11." As I will show you, the oldest Bible in Greek marks both of these passages, as well as 1 Corinthians 14:34–35, as later additions. Many scholars have concluded that 14:34–35 was not in Paul's original letter.[52]

Allow me to show you some of the evidence so you can decide for yourself. This section will delve into the art and science of determining the original text of the Bible, but I will try to keep it as simple as possible.

One strong evidence that these two verses were not in Paul's original text is the fact that they appear in two significantly different locations in early manuscripts. Every version of the Bible that you have likely read (including the NIV, ESV, and KJV) is based primarily on what are called the "Alexandrian text-type" or "Byzantine text-type" manuscripts. In most of these manuscripts, this passage follows immediately after verse 33. However, another group of old manuscripts contains what is called the "Western" text. In these manuscripts, this passage comes at the end of 1 Corinthians 14, right after verse 40. We are not just talking about a few insignificant manuscripts, but the entire textual tradition known as the "Western" Greek text. Here is an example of this passage from the best-known of the "Western" manuscripts, *Codex Claromontanus D* (06) from the sixth century:

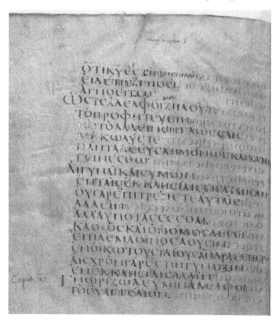

Reproduced under license from Bibliothèque nationale de France

52. Payne, *Man and Woman, One in Christ*, 226–227 identifies fifty-five studies that conclude that 14:34–35 was not in Paul's original letter.

The first paragraph at the top of the image is 1 Corinthians 14:39–40, followed by 14:34–35 as a separate paragraph, followed by "Caput XV" (chapter 15) in the margin next to a new paragraph beginning with 15:1.

The question, therefore, is: What could explain why this passage occurs in two different positions this far apart in different manuscripts? There are three possibilities:

1. It was originally after verse 33, and someone moved it to follow verse 40.

2. It was originally after verse 40, and someone moved it to follow verse 33.

3. Someone wrote it in the margin, and later scribes put it in the text where they thought it fit best, either after verse 33 or after verse 40.

There are many documented instances of insertions copied into the body text from text written in the margin, but there is no case in any manuscript of any of Paul's letters where a passage this long was moved to a location this far away without an obvious reason. This makes possibilities (1) and (2) unprecedented, and consequently, highly unlikely.

When scribes were creating a new copy of a manuscript, it was common for them to insert into the main text any words they found in the margin. The fourth-century Codex Vaticanus, commonly referred to simply as "Vaticanus," demonstrates this convention. Vaticanus contains twenty instances of small readable old text in the margins of Matthew. All but three of them are found in the main text of virtually every surviving subsequent manuscript.

Only the third possibility fits known scribal conventions and only it provides a natural explanation why 14:34–35 occurs in these two locations. Consequently, it is most likely that 1 Corinthians 14:34–35 was first written in the margin and that one or more scribes inserted the marginal comment after verse 33, explaining its usual position, and another scribe (or scribes) inserted it after verse 40, resulting in its "Western" position. These are the only two reasonable insertion points in this vicinity. Because this is a unique case with no close parallel in any manuscript of Paul's letters, it does not undermine the authenticity of any other passage.

Another evidence that 14:34–35 was added later is that Vaticanus marks it as a later addition.[53] Most current scholars consider Vaticanus to be one of the best Greek texts of the New Testament.[54] It is the earliest manuscript that includes most of the Bible (Old and New Testament). It has been in the Vatican (hence its name) since the fifteenth century. The Vaticanus New Testament and its Old Testament prophetic books were penned by the same scribe, identified by scholars as "scribe B." Before we look at these verses in 1 Corinthians 14, let me illustrate this from a different verse, Matthew 18:11. I encourage you to look up Matthew 18:10–12 in your Bible:

> *See that you do not despise one of these little ones. For I tell you that their angels in heaven always see the face of my Father in heaven.* (Matthew 18:10) *What do you think? If a man owns a hundred sheep, and one of them wanders away, will he not leave the ninety-nine on the hills and go to look for the one that wandered off?* (Matthew 18:12)

Notice something missing? Right, there is no Matthew 18:11! What does your Bible show? Depending on your translation, it might have a special footnote, or be printed in italics or in square brackets. Most recent Bible versions do not include Matthew 18:11 because it is not in the earliest manuscripts and does not fit the natural flow of the text here. The vast majority of scholars have concluded that it was not part of the original text of Matthew but was inserted from Luke 19:10, where it flows naturally following the salvation of the tax collector Zacchaeus: "*For the Son of Man came to seek and to save the lost.*"

---

53. Philip B. Payne, "Vaticanus Distigme-obelos Symbols Marking Added Text, Including 1 Corinthians 14.34–5", *NTS* 63 (2017) 604–625, downloadable free at https://www.cambridge.org/core/journals/new-testament-studies/article/vaticanus-distigmeobelos-symbols-marking-added-text-including-1-corinthians-14345/A5FC01A6E14A2A1CF1F514A9BF93C581.

54. Wikipedia, online at https://en.wikipedia.org/wiki/Codex_Vaticanus.

Now, look at this verse as it is written in Vaticanus. I added the triangle to show where Matthew 18:11 was added later but is not in Vaticanus:

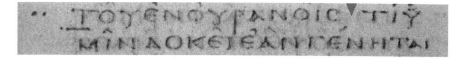

Four features in Vaticanus together specify that verse 11 was not in Matthew's original text:

1. Two dots (called a "distigme") in the left margin mark the location where other manuscripts have a different text (called a "textual variant"), as they do throughout Vaticanus.[55]

2. A horizontal bar (called an "obelos") marks where text was added.[56]

3. The obelos is located below and to the right of the distigme.

4. A gap in the text on that same line (highlighted by my triangle) marks the precise location where a later insertion interrupted the text of Matthew.

The only added text at this gap with any manuscript evidence is verse 11.

We know it was scribe B who made these marks because only scribe B could leave a gap in the original text (later scribes could not move text that was already there), and parts of some of these marks were not reinked with the rest of the manuscript in the Middle Ages, so they still have the same apricot color as the original Vaticanus ink. There are fifteen places in the New Testament where scribe B added these "distigme-obelos" symbols. Each has a gap at the exact location the original text was interrupted. Additions this long occur, on

---

55. Philip B. Payne and Paul Canart, "Distigmai Matching the Original Ink of *Codex Vaticanus*: Do They Mark the Location of Textual Variants?" in *Le manuscrit B de la Bible (Vaticanus graecus 1209), Introduction au fac-similé, Actes du Colloque de Genève (11 juin 2001), Contributions supplémentaire* (Patrick Andrist, ed.; HTB 7; Lausanne: Éditions du Zèbre, 2009) 199–226, downloadable at **www.pbpayne.com** under Publications: Articles.

56. Vaticanus obelos bars extend farther into the margin and are longer than most undisputed distigme-line paragraph bars. We know that Paragraph bars were not originally in the Vaticanus New Testament because none match its original ink color. See Payne, "Distigme-obelos", 618–621, 614.

average, only once every 83.5 lines of Vaticanus text.[57] Consequently, for this to occur on every Vaticanus line with a distigme-obelos cannot plausibly be attributed to chance.

Finally, we know that scribe B intended these horizontal bars to mark locations where text was added because scribe B explained three times in Isaiah that a horizontal bar obelos marks lines where Vaticanus's Greek text adds words that were not in the Hebrew Scriptures. Here is the original image of the one at Isaiah 51:23 (I added the annotation):

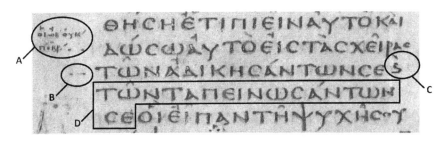

A. Note the small letters in the left margin: ΟΙⲰΒ΄ΟΥΚ΄Π΄ΕΒρ΄. This is scribe B's abbreviation for οἱ ὠβελίσμενοι οὐ κεῖται παρ᾽ ἑβραίοις. It means "the [text] marked with an obelos does not occur in [the] Hebrew [text]." It corresponds to the distigme (two-dot abbreviation) since it also marks the location of a textual variant.

B. Below and to the right of that abbreviated explanation (A) you can see a horizontal bar obelos by a line with a gap in the text.

C. The gap is at the end of the line on the right side. The darker, accented "S" (a symbol for "and") was added by a later scribe. If you imagine removing that accented "S," that is where the gap is.

D. The gap marks the location where the Greek translation added words not found in the Hebrew: τῶν ταπεινωσάντων σε ("them that humbled you"). The added words fill the next line and continue onto the following line. As you see, early Greek manuscripts do not contain spaces between words.

---

57. All of these additions are widely acknowledged and add four or more consecutive words. See https://www.pbpayne.com/wp-content/uploads/2021/07/Critique-of-Fellows-Krans-Vaticanus-Distigme-Obelos-Denials.pdf.

With that background, here is 1 Corinthians 14:34–35 in Vaticanus (I added the triangle):

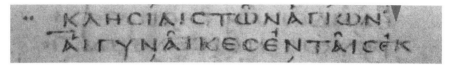

As you can see, the four previously mentioned features are present (repeated here):

1. A two-dot distigme.

2. A horizontal bar obelos.

3. The obelos is below and to the right of the distigme.

4. There is a gap at the end of that line of text at the precise point where the original text was interrupted. That interruption, 1 Corinthians 14:34–35, is widely recognized to be a later addition.

The combination of these four features makes it clear that the gap marks where the original text was interrupted. The only added text at this gap with any manuscript support is 1 Corinthians 14:34–35. As in Isaiah 51:23, the gap at the end of 1 Corinthians 14:33 separates the original text from the added text (1 Corinthians 14:34–35) on the following lines.

Why should we trust scribe B's judgment that 1 Corinthians 14:34–35 was not in Paul's original letter? First, we should trust scribe B because scribe B had access to far more pre-Vaticanus manuscript text than we have today.[58] And second, both standard editions of the Greek New Testament and virtually all modern translations agree with scribe B that every other added block of text marked by a distigme-obelos was not in the original text of Scripture. Consequently, their texts do not include any of these additions. Since scholarship has confirmed that scribe B was correct in every other case, 1 Corinthians 14:34–35 should also be considered a later addition.

---

58. This is evident from the wide variety of manuscripts that contain the added text marked by the distigme-obelos symbols and the textual variants marked by original ink Vaticanus distigmai.

Because of all this evidence, I find it compelling that 1 Corinthians 14:34–35 was not in Paul's original letter and should not be considered part of the Bible.

Galatians 3:28: Man and Woman, One in Christ[59]

Galatians 2:4–14 explains that Jews in Galatia were pressuring gentile Christians to conform to Jewish laws. Even Peter was refusing to eat with gentiles when Jews were present. Paul rebukes Peter for this. In Galatians 3:28, Paul gives the theological foundation for his repudiation of Peter's actions:

> *There is neither Jew nor Gentile, neither slave nor free, nor is there male and female, for you are all one in Christ Jesus.* (Galatians 3:28)

Galatians 3:28 asserts a radically new understanding of relationships in Christ—one without any division between Jew and Greek, slave and free, and male and female. Obviously, this doesn't indicate that everyone is identical or that all do the same thing. But what does Paul mean when he says that there is no male and female in Christ?

One secret to understanding this passage is Paul's usage of the Greek conjunction *oude*. He uses this between Jew and Greek and between slave and free to join two elements to convey a single idea.[60] Paul must not mean that "there is no Jew *nor* Greek in Christ" because there are Jews in Christ and there are Greeks in Christ. Instead, Paul through each pair makes a single point that is better translated that in Christ "there is no Jew-Greek division, no slave-free division, and no male-female division."

Oude joins two elements to convey a single idea in most of the places Paul uses it, including 2 Thessalonians 3:7–8:

> *For you yourselves know how you ought to follow our example. We were not idle when we were with you, nor* (oude) *did we eat anyone's*

---

59. For further discussion, see Payne, *Man and Woman, One in Christ*, 79–104.
60. Philip B. Payne, "1 Timothy 2.12 and the Use of οὐδέ to Combine Two Elements to Express a Single Idea", NTS 54 (2008) 235–253; Philip B. Payne, "Οὐδέ Combining Two Elements to Convey a Single Idea and 1 Timothy 2:12", *Missing Voices: Broadening the Discussion on Men, Women, and Ministry* (ed. Hilary Ritchie; Minneapolis: CBE International, 2014) 24–34.

food without paying for it. On the contrary, we worked night and day,
laboring and toiling so that we would not be a burden to any of you.
(2 Thessalonians 3:7–8)

The NIV text gives the impression that Paul is saying two things: he was not idle and he paid every one of his hosts for the food he ate. But Paul chooses the conjunction *oude*, which he uses elsewhere to combine two things to make a single point. It would have insulted Paul's hosts for him to pay them for the food they gave him. There is no shame in eating food that is given to you— that is simply accepting hospitality. And there is no shame in resting. But there is shame in freeloading. As Paul's following sentence explains, it is the combination of being idle and eating free food that Paul disavows here. It is more accurately translated: "In our stay with you, we were not idle while eating anyone's food without paying for it."

Returning to "male and female" in Galatians 3:28, Paul does not use the word *oude* but uses a different conjunction, *kai* ("and"). However, the substitution of *kai* for *oude* does not indicate a difference in meaning for "male-female" from that for "Jew-Greek" or "slave-free."[61] We know that Paul intended all three pairs to be viewed in the same way because of the "all" in his explanation: *"for you are all one in Christ Jesus."* This must apply to all three of the prior pairs, including male and female. Also, the surrounding statements, *"you are all children of God through faith"* (3:26) and *"you are Abraham's seed, and heirs according to the promise"* (3:29), are inclusive of all believers and so affirm the same status and privileges for women as for men.

Galatians 3:28 teaches that male-female division does not exist in Christ. This means that we must not restrict privilege in Christ's church based on the categories of male and female. Paul's point is that gender, just like race and social rank, is irrelevant to status in Christ. Just like gentiles should be included in the church with the same privileges as Jews, and slaves should be included in

---

61. Paul is simply continuing the list of contrasting groups of people, while using the standard conjunction that is used to describe God's creation of *"male and female"* (e.g., Genesis 1:27; 5:2; Matthew 19:4; Mark 10:6). Paul similarly substitutes *kai* for *oude* to teach the same single idea in Romans 10:12, *"there is no difference between Jew and* (kai) *Gentile."*

the church with the same privileges as free persons, so also women should be included in the church with the same privileges as men.

Exclusion of all women from church leadership or teaching is precisely the sort of restriction of privilege that Galatians 3:28 repudiates.

In Galatians 2:13–14, Paul calls Peter a "hypocrite" and says he is "acting contrary to the gospel" for withdrawing from table fellowship with gentiles. It is at least as contrary to the gospel and to our oneness in Christ to exclude all women from church leadership and from teaching men. The barriers that separate male and female in society do not exist in the new reality of being one in Christ. It is contrary to the plain meaning of "there is no male-female division in the body of Christ" to say that there is a male-female division in the body of Christ with all females barred from church leadership and from teaching men.

GALATIANS 3: ANSWER TO THE ONE COMMON OBJECTION

"Galatians 3:28 is not about divisions in the church and the family but is only talking about who can be saved."

There is really only one common objection, that Paul is not talking about life on earth but only about who can be saved. But is Galatians 3:28 talking only about who can be saved? No, I don't think so! Each of the three relationships mentioned in this verse specifically relates to social standing, so to say that they have nothing to do with social standing is to deny their most obvious application. The book of Galatians is largely about actual, physical, earthly disputes between Jews and gentiles.

Recall that in the first part of Galatians, we learn that Peter had stopped eating with gentiles in Galatia. But Paul *"opposed him to his face, because he stood condemned . . . [of] hypocrisy . . . [and] not acting in line with the truth of the gospel"* (Galatians 2:11–14). In defending Paul's denunciation of Peter's unequal treatment of Jews and gentiles, Galatians 3:28 affirms the equality of Jew and gentile in Christ and expands it to include slave and free and male and female.

Theo, if this verse did not mention male-female division in Christ, then no one would try to limit its application to who can be saved. After all, when Paul expresses almost the exact same thought in Colossians, it is unmistakable that he is talking about life here on earth in Christian fellowship:

> *Here there is no Gentile or Jew, circumcised or uncircumcised, barbarian, Scythian, slave or free, but Christ is all, and is in all. Therefore, as God's chosen people, holy and dearly loved, clothe yourselves with compassion, kindness, humility, gentleness and patience.* (Colossians 3:11–12)

And when Paul mentions similar thoughts later in Galatians, we all understand that he is talking about life here on earth in Christian fellowship:

> *For in Christ Jesus neither circumcision nor uncircumcision has any value. The only thing that counts is faith expressing itself through love.* (Galatians 5:6)

> *Neither circumcision nor uncircumcision means anything; what counts is the new creation.* (Galatians 6:15)

When Paul talks about breaking down barriers between the circumcised and uncircumcised in Ephesians, we all understand that he is talking about life here on earth in Christian fellowship:

> *For he himself is our peace, who has made the two groups one and has destroyed the barrier, the dividing wall of hostility . . .* (Ephesians 2:14)

> *Consequently, you are no longer foreigners and strangers, but fellow citizens with God's people and also members of his household,* (Ephesians 2:19)

And when Paul similarly talks about baptism into the body of Christ in 1 Corinthians, we all understand that he is talking about life here on earth in Christian fellowship:

> *Just as a body, though one, has many parts, but all its many parts form one body, so it is with Christ. For we were all baptized by one Spirit so*

as to form one body—whether Jews or Gentiles, slave or free—and we were all given the one Spirit to drink. (1 Corinthians 12:12–13)

But for some reason, as soon as Paul adds the relationship between male and female, some people think he cannot possibly be talking about here and now; he must be talking only about salvation in God's sight. But in addition to this interpretation contradicting all Paul's parallel passages, many other reasons also lead us to conclude that Galatians 3:28 does affect life here on earth in Christian fellowship:

- There was no dispute about salvation. As far as we know, they didn't dispute whether gentiles, slaves, or women could become Christians, so there is no reason for Paul to suddenly need to affirm that they can be saved.

- "One in Christ" refers to community. When Paul mentions that we are "one in Christ," or "all one body," he is referring to relationships between people in the body of Christ, the church; he is not speaking only of each individual's spiritual state before God. In Christ, "oneness" replaces racial, social, and biological divisions. Consequently, discrimination and special privilege based on these external factors are contrary to the unity of Christ's body, the new humanity where Jews and gentiles share equal citizenship (cf. 1 Corinthians 12:12–13; Ephesians 2:11–22; Colossians 3:10–11).

- The theme of radical newness of life in Christ permeates Galatians. Galatians 1:4; 2:20, "I no longer live, but Christ lives in me." Galatians 3:2, 5, 14, "Receive the promise of the Spirit." Galatians 4:3, 5–7, "you are no longer a slave, but God's child . . . an heir." Galatians 5:19–24, "Those who belong to Christ Jesus have crucified the flesh and its passions and desires." Galatians 5:25–26, "Since we live by the Spirit, let us keep step with the Spirit." Galatians 6:15 affirms "the new creation." To interpret Galatians 3:28 as having nothing to do with relationships or as too extreme to be taken literally is incompatible with this radical newness of life here on earth that Paul affirms.

- Denial of divisions in Christ. The entire book of Galatians is a frontal attack against favored status or privileges being granted to Jews over gentiles. In this context, 3:28's "There is no Jew-Greek division . . . in Christ" denies any exclusion of gentiles from any privilege or position in the church. The absence in Christ of the distinction between Jew and gentile is the foundation on which Paul denies the need for circumcision, the central practical issue of Galatians,[62] so Galatians 3:28 must not be restricted to spiritual status.

- Galatians stresses freedom from the law in Christ. Galatians 2:4 and following describes Paul's opposition to *"false believers* [who] *had infiltrated our ranks to spy on the freedom we have in Christ Jesus and to make us slaves."* Galatians 3:23–25 affirms, *"we were held in custody under the law, locked up . . . Now that this faith has come we are no longer under a guardian."* Galatians 5:1 asserts, *"It is for freedom that Christ has set us free. Stand firm, then, and do not let yourselves be burdened again by a yoke of slavery."* This freedom from the law is not just about salvation in heaven but has huge implications for life in the church.

- In Galatians 3:28, Paul is probably refuting a common Jewish prayer found repeatedly in early Jewish literature, "Blessed art Thou, O Lord our God, King of the Universe, who hast not made me a heathen . . . a bondman . . . [or] a woman."[63] According to rabbinic tradition, these three groups were excluded from the study of the law. Paul's denial of these exclusions must therefore require the inclusion of Greeks, slaves, and women in the privilege of studying the law in the actual life of the church.

In summary, Galatians 3:28 is a call to radically new social interaction based on equality in the body of Christ, the church, here on earth. Without any hint that there are exceptions, it states that in Christ there is no male-female division.

---

62. Cf. the references to circumcision in Galatians 2:3, 7, 8, 9, 12; 5:2, 3, 6, 11; 6:12, 13, 15.

63. George S. Duncan, *The Epistle of Paul to the Galatians* (London: Hodder and Stoughton, 1934) 123.

Ephesians 5:21–33:
Husband-Wife Mutual Submission[64]

Okay, it's time to discuss Ephesians—Paul's second-longest passage regarding husbands and wives (after 1 Corinthians 7). It has also inspired at least one popular wedding song!

Submit to one another out of reverence for Christ.

Wives, submit yourselves to your own husbands as you do to the Lord. For the husband is the head of the wife as Christ is the head of the church, his body, of which he is the Savior. Now as the church submits to Christ, so also wives should submit to their husbands in everything.

Husbands, love your wives, just as Christ loved the church and gave himself up for her to make her holy, cleansing her by the washing with water through the word, and to present her to himself as a radiant church, without stain or wrinkle or any other blemish, but holy and blameless. In this same way, husbands ought to love their wives as their own bodies. He who loves his wife loves himself. After all, no one ever hated their own body, but they feed and care for their body, just as Christ does the church—for we are members of his body. "For this reason a man will leave his father and mother and be united to his wife, and the two will become one flesh." This is a profound mystery—but I am talking about Christ and the church. However, each one of you also must love his wife as he loves himself, and the wife must respect her husband. (Ephesians 5:21–33)

Theo, in the second paragraph as quoted above, you will see it says something about wives submitting to their husbands in everything, just like they submit to Christ! And if you are not careful when you read it, your brain might start to go into a fog and cause you to see things that aren't really there, like:

---

64. For further discussion, see Payne, *Man and Woman, One in Christ,* 271–290.

In this passage, Paul compares the marriage relationship to that of Christ and the church. Within the power dynamics of a marriage, Paul says that husbands are like Christ, and wives are—well, it doesn't matter—they are *not* like Christ. Wives should choose to submit themselves to their husbands. That might sound like advice, not a command, but it is advice from God, so it is essentially a command. So, women must submit to husbands in absolutely everything just like they submit to Christ because, well, husbands are like Christ. And since I am a husband and Christ is God, therefore, I am pretty much God. Okay, not exactly God, but much more like God than my wife is. Wow, this is awesome! Even better than being Batman! And sure, Paul tells me to love my wife. But the main point Paul makes is that I am, for all practical purposes, God over my wife. No more having to discuss stuff (unless I want to), no more having to explain myself (unless I want to), no more having to do the dishes (unless I want to) . . .

snaps out of it

Sorry, Theo, I got lost in a dream. Wow, this is not merely a slippery slope! It is more like a black hole, sucking in all who would get close to it!

I know it appears to many that God is giving husbands unilateral authority over their submitting wives. But, no, that is not what Paul is saying at all. Let's start by considering two key verses from this chapter:

> *Follow God's example, therefore, as dearly loved children and walk in the way of love, just as Christ loved us and gave himself up for us as a fragrant offering and sacrifice to God.* (Ephesians 5:1–2)

> *Submit to one another out of reverence for Christ.* (Ephesians 5:21)

In the first one, "*Walk in the way of love*" simply means to love one another, and to do so "*as Christ loved us and gave himself up for us.*" This means we are all called to love one another with a perfect, selfless, sacrificial love. Consequently, this chapter commands both husbands and wives to love each other *as Christ loved us and gave himself up for us.* Therefore it is a mistake to think that Christ is the model for husbands in a way that he is not for the wife. Christ's loving sacrifice is the model for both wives and husbands. The second one says to *submit to one another.* That includes men and women, and husbands and wives.

The sentence that includes Ephesians 5:22 starts at 5:18 when Paul commands all believers: *"Instead, be filled with the Holy Spirit,"* and then he gives examples of what people do who are filled with the Spirit:

- *speaking to one another with psalms, hymns, and songs from the Spirit, singing and making music from your heart to the Lord* (Ephesians 5:19)

- *giving thanks always to God the Father for everything in the name of our Lord Jesus Christ* (Ephesians 5:20)

- *submitting to one another out of reverence of Christ* (Ephesians 5:21).

There is no verb in Ephesians 5:22. That verse gets its verb from 5:21's *"submit to one another."* This means that 5:22 is a continuation of the sentence from 5:21. Both standard editions of the Greek New Testament show that 5:22 is part of the sentence including 5:21. The command that wives submit to their husbands, therefore, should be understood in the light of mutual submission. Many translations, including the NIV, separate Paul's single sentence into three separate paragraphs, even inserting a paragraph break between verses 21 and 22. This butchers Paul's interconnected logic and obscures how closely Paul links wives' submission in Ephesians 5:22 to mutual submission.

Paul is calling wives to submit to their husbands, but he makes it clear that the wives' submission is in the context of the mutual submission of believers to each other. I, too, affirm that wives should submit to their husbands, but like Paul, I affirm it as part of the mutual submission that requires that husbands should also submit to their wives.

However, the mutual submission between husband and wife is not like the standard mutual submission between all Christians. A husband and wife have formed one flesh, and as one flesh, they uniquely demonstrate the oneness of mutual submission. As such, the mutual submission between husband and wife is much, much more intense and intimate.

Wives are to surrender their lives to their husbands and submit to them in everything. The idea of total submission sounds scary to us today because we know how much it can be abused. But Paul does not have to give wives any more instructions about this because it was already part of the patriarchal Greco-Roman rules at the time that gave husbands the final authority in the household. Husbands, on the other hand, were not accustomed to submitting, so they have no idea what's about to hit them in the next paragraph.

Husbands have a responsibility also—they must love their wives. I know this sounds like a horribly unfair exchange at first—total submission versus a bit of love—and husbands may momentarily think that they are getting off easy. But let's dig a bit deeper. Just how much are husbands supposed to love their wives? An insanely outrageous amount! Paul says husbands are to love their wives as much as "Christ loved the church and gave himself up for her." That phrase, "gave himself up," refers to Christ surrendering his life. He died for his church. You can see the same phrase used many times in the New Testament referring to Christ, including:

> I have been crucified with Christ and I no longer live, but Christ lives in me. The life I now live in the body, I live by faith in the Son of God, who loved me and **gave himself** for me. (Galatians 2:20)

How did Christ make the church holy? He died. How did Christ cleanse the church, removing all stains, wrinkles, and blemishes? He died on the cross! How did Christ make the church blameless? He surrendered his life, giving it up for the church. And Paul is telling husbands that they must do likewise.

But Paul is not simply telling husbands to be "willing" to surrender their lives just in case, as in the defender or protector of their wives. Like if the two of them were attacked by a grizzly bear or a pack of wolves, the husband would jump in front and defend his wife even if he died in the process. While that is certainly honorable of the husband, it is not what Paul is saying. Christ was not merely the "bodyguard" of the church. Paul is saying that husbands must *actually* surrender their lives to their wives. That is what Christ *actually* did for you and me, the church, because Christ *actually* loved us that much.

Wives are to fully surrender their lives to their husbands. Husbands are to fully surrender their lives to their wives. That is the crazy intense level of mutual submission that Paul is calling husbands and wives to. And as radical and crazy as it sounds, it should also sound a little familiar because that is exactly what Paul said earlier in 1 Corinthians:

> *The wife does not have authority over her own body but yields it to her husband. In the same way, the husband does not have authority over his own body but yields it to his wife.* (1 Corinthians 7:4)

Theo, you might have thought Paul was only talking about physical intimacy within marriage, but Paul had bigger ideas in mind. Paul is telling each of them that they need to give up control of their lives to the other person. That is what it means to become "one flesh"—nothing less than total and complete mutual submission.

After presenting this truth, Paul reminds husbands that they are "*united*" and "*one flesh*" (Ephesians 5:31) with their wives and gives practical advice about what that means for husbands to surrender themselves to their wives, contrary to the culture of the day. Although becoming "*one flesh*" will look different for each husband, one thing will remain consistent:

> *In this same way, husbands ought to love their wives as their own bodies. He who loves his wife loves himself.* (Ephesians 5:28)

> *However, each one of you also must love his wife as he loves himself* . . . (Ephesians 5:33)

As these verses state, each husband must love his wife as much he loves himself. This is a profound teaching, except haven't we heard this before? Like at the beginning of Ephesians 5? And pretty much everywhere in the Bible from Old Testament to New Testament?

> *Do not seek revenge or bear a grudge against anyone among your people, but love your neighbor as yourself. I am the LORD.* (Leviticus 19:18)

> *The second is this: "Love your neighbor as yourself." There is no commandment greater than these.* (Mark 12:31)

> *For the entire law is fulfilled in keeping this one command: "Love your neighbor as yourself."* (Galatians 5:14)

So, husbands must surrender their lives to their wives. And all those Bible passages about loving your neighbor as yourself really do apply to husbands as well.

EPHESIANS 5: ANSWERS TO COMMON OBJECTIONS

With that in mind, Theo, let me respond to a couple of common objections.

"Whatever mutual submission exists is not symmetrical. Ephesians 5:23 says the husband is the head of the wife, which means he is in charge."

It does say that the husband is the head of the wife, as Christ is the head of the church. But in contrast to English, "authority" was not an established meaning of "head" in the Greek of Paul's day. I previously discussed the definition of "head" in the section on 1 Corinthians 11 and mentioned that Paul usually uses it to mean "source." Here Paul uses parallel expressions to explain what he means by "head": "Christ head of the church, he savior of the body." The NIV was wrong to conceal this "emphatic" explanation.[65] Paul explains what he means by "head" here, namely that Christ saved the church by giving his life for the church. Christ does have authority over the church, but that is not what Paul explains "head" to mean here. Paul explains, instead, that Christ is

---

65. A. T. Robertson, *A Grammar of the Greek New Testament in the Light of Historical Research* (Nashville, TN: Broadman, 1934) 399 "emphatic apposition." All references to "Savior" as a title of Christ are in later literature. This and the absence of an article support the translation, "savior."

the "source" of the life of the church. This is also what Paul means by "head" earlier in Ephesians:

> *Instead, speaking the truth in love, we will grow to become in every respect the mature body of him who is the head, that is, Christ. From him the whole body, joined and held together by every supporting ligament, grows and builds itself up in love, as each part does its work.* (Ephesians 4:15–16)

Because the head is the source "from whom" the body "grows," clearly Paul meant "head" to mean "source" here. This is also the meaning of "head" in other passages in Paul's letters, including 1 Corinthians 11:3, as we have already seen, and in these verses:

> *They have lost connection with the head, from whom the whole body, supported and held together by its ligaments and sinews, grows as God causes it to grow.* (Colossians 2:19)

> *And he is the head of the body, the church; he is the beginning* (archē, meaning source). (Colossians 1:18)

Paul goes on to explain what Christ did as savior of the body: "*Christ loved the church and gave himself up for her*" and "nourishes and cherishes" her. As head, Christ is the church's savior, its source of life, love, and nourishment. Husbands as "head" are to *"love your wives, just as Christ loved the church and gave himself up for her"* (verse 25) and to "nourish and cherish" them *"just as Christ does the church"* (verse 29).

One can even say that as Christ is the source of life for the church, the husband, in that culture, was the source of life for his wife since he provided all that was essential for her to live. The aspect of "head" that this passage develops is a call for husbands to love, give themselves for, nourish, and cherish their wives just as Christ as "head" is the source of all these for the church. Ephesians 5 does not tell husbands to have authority over their wives, but rather "*to submit to one another,*" a command to the whole church that Paul specifically applies first to wives in verses 22–24 and then to husbands in verses 25–33.

> **"But '*submitting to one another*' is equally applied to all believers, and specifically children to fathers and slaves to masters; Paul is not trying to eliminate a father's authority over his children—likewise, Paul is not trying to eliminate the authority of husbands over their wives."**

Ephesians affirms mutual submission in the church and in husband-wife relationships, but not regarding either children or slaves. I am not saying that mutual submission in the body of Christ has no bearing on parent-child or master-slave relations. I am saying that husband and wife, as one flesh, uniquely demonstrate the oneness of mutual submission. Consequently, Paul did not need to write any verb in verse 22. The mutual submission mentioned in verse 21 applies perfectly to wives and husbands. However, the following passages about children and slaves use a different verb, "obey," which is a very specific command, much different than mutual submission, best understood as "voluntary yielding in love."[66]

---

66. BDAG 1042.

Colossians 3:18–4:1: Submission Revisited[67]

In Colossians, we find instructions regarding submission in marriage similar to those given in Ephesians:

> *Wives, submit yourselves to your husbands, as is fitting in the Lord. Husbands, love your wives and do not be harsh with them.*
> (Colossians 3:18–19)

At first glance, these commands seem like other verses telling wives to submit to their husbands and for husbands to love their wives. However, in every other instance when the Bible tells wives to submit to their husbands, it either:

1. Calls for mutual submission between husbands and wives
   (1 Corinthians 7, Ephesians 5, and 1 Peter 3) or

2. Explains that the reason for wives' submission is to fit into the surrounding culture so as not to impede spreading the gospel (Titus 2:5, 1 Peter 3:1).

But here we find neither of those. So, how should we understand these verses? Since Paul wrote Colossians, we should not interpret these verses in a way that conflicts with his fuller statements regarding mutual submission in 1 Corinthians 7 and Ephesians 5.

One helpful insight is to look at how Colossians talks about slaves. Early in Colossians 3, we find Paul describing how the Christian community should be:

> *Here there is no Gentile or Jew, circumcised or uncircumcised, barbarian, Scythian, slave or free, but Christ is all, and is in all.*
> (Colossians 3:11)

---

67. For further discussion, see Payne, *Man and Woman, One in Christ*, 271–277.

And this is not merely a peek into what life will be like in heaven. No, Paul is talking about life here on earth in Christian fellowship, as can be seen in the verses which follow:

> *Therefore, as God's chosen people, holy and dearly loved, clothe your-selves with compassion, kindness, humility, gentleness and patience. Bear with each other and forgive one another if any of you has a grievance against someone. Forgive as the Lord forgave you. And over all these virtues put on love, which binds them all together in perfect unity. Let the peace of Christ rule in your hearts, since as members of one body you were called to peace. And be thankful. Let the mes-sage of Christ dwell among you richly as you teach and admonish one another with all wisdom through psalms, hymns, and songs from the Spirit, singing to God with gratitude in your hearts. And whatever you do, whether in word or deed, do it all in the name of the Lord Jesus, giving thanks to God the Father through him.* (Colossians 3:12–17)

Like mutual submission, "one another" is reciprocal. And being taught and accepting admonishment by someone else entails submission. Furthermore, both Colossians 3:25 and Ephesians 6:9 conclude *"there is no favoritism."* So both the introduction and conclusion of these passages emphasize the equal standing of all who are in Christ.

Therefore, within Christian fellowship, there should be no distinction between slave or free. This should sound very familiar since Paul says the same thing in Galatians 3:28 and 1 Corinthians 12:13. Yet, just a few verses later, we find this command:

> *Slaves, obey your earthly masters in everything; and do it, not only when their eye is on you and to curry their favor, but with sincerity of heart and reverence for the Lord.* (Colossians 3:22)

On the one hand, there should be no distinction between slave and free. But on the other hand, slaves are supposed to obey their masters in everything. So there should be no slavery *and* slaves should obey their masters? Theo, I trust you see the problem here. Before you read on, I urge you to take a minute to go back and forth between those two verses, stare at them a while, and reflect on their difference.

Don't get me wrong—Paul's instructions for households are good. Paul, in addressing the patriarchal rules of that time, requires those in authority to give deference to those under them:

- *Husbands, love your wives and do not be harsh with them.* (Colossians 3:19 This explicitly prohibits wife abuse.)

- *Fathers, do not embitter your children* . . . (Colossians 3:21)

- *Masters, provide your slaves with what is right and fair* (Colossians 4:1 more precisely: "give justice and equality to your slaves").

We need to be sensitive to Paul's audience, whether slaves with harsh masters or believing slave owners. But we also need to distinguish "God's desire for how we should live" from "What God has allowed to happen," and most notably here: "How to make the best out of what God has allowed to happen." While Paul's instructions to slaves to submit to their masters are practical (since being a good slave was the best way to gain freedom), 3:11–17 makes it clear that slavery is not the ideal we should be striving for. To find God's ideal for slavery, we need to look in the earlier verses listed above, Colossians 3:8–17, which states slavery does not exist in Christ and that all Christians should treat each other with compassion, kindness, humility, gentleness, and patience, bearing with each other, forgiving each other, and loving each other.

Similarly, instructions for households in Colossians 3:18 do not describe the full picture of God's ideal for husbands and wives. Rather, God's ideal comes from the same earlier verses, Colossians 3:8–17, which describe a loving mutual submission among all believers. But to find statements that specifically discuss God's ideal for husbands and wives, you should go to one of Paul's other passages listed above, like Ephesians 5 and 1 Corinthians 7, which contain more complete and precise descriptions of how husbands and wives should relate to each other.

1 Timothy 2:
A Woman Assuming Authority to Teach a Man[68]

Wow, Theo, can you believe it? We have finally made our way to 1 Timothy! This will definitely take me a few sections to get through.

WHAT'S THE PROBLEM?

The first full paragraph of 1 Timothy and the content of both it and 2 Timothy show that Paul is writing to Timothy to advise him on dealing with false teaching in the church at Ephesus. Remember that Paul helped start this church in Ephesus (Acts 18–20) and warned the elders when he left:

> *I know that after I leave, savage wolves will come in among you and will not spare the flock. Even from your own number men will arise and distort the truth in order to draw away disciples after them. So be on your guard! Remember that for three years I never stopped warning each of you night and day with tears.* (Acts 20:29–31)

And, sure enough, the main problem Paul addresses is false teaching. But he differentiates between those who were false teachers because they were ignorant and those who were willfully blasphemous. For example, Paul himself was a false teacher, but he was ignorant, as he confesses:

> *Even though I was once a blasphemer and a persecutor and a violent man, I was shown mercy because I acted in ignorance and unbelief … But for that very reason I was shown mercy so that in me, the worst of sinners, Christ Jesus might display his immense patience as an example for those who would believe in him and receive eternal life.* (1 Timothy 1:13, 16)

---

68. For further discussion, see Payne, *Man and Woman, One in Christ*, 291–310.

On the other hand, Paul names two specific teachers in Ephesus who were knowingly spreading false teachings:

> *Timothy, my son, I am giving you this command in keeping with the prophecies once made about you, so that by recalling them you may fight the battle well, holding on to faith and a good conscience, which some have rejected and so have suffered shipwreck with regard to the faith. Among them are Hymenaeus and Alexander, whom I have handed over to Satan to be taught not to blaspheme.* (1 Timothy 1:18–20)

Those who blaspheme knowingly are to be rejected. These include Hymenaeus and Alexander, whom Paul has already *"handed over to Satan"* (1:20). But the rest of 1 Timothy deals primarily with those who had been deceived by the blasphemous teachers and were themselves spreading false teachings out of ignorance. Misinformed teachers, whom Paul identifies as women, were deceived by the blasphemous teachers. But how do we know that women were involved in continuing the false teaching?

First, whenever Paul describes the false teachers collectively, he consistently uses the Greek word *tis*, meaning "someone" or "anyone." For example:

- *that you may command certain people* (tis) *not to teach false doctrines any longer . . .* (1 Timothy 1:3)

- *some* (tis) *have departed from these . . .* (1 Timothy 1:6)

- *holding on to faith and a good conscience, which some* (tis) *have rejected . . .* (1 Timothy 1:19)

If all the false teachers were men, then Paul would probably have used masculine terms to describe them. The fact that Paul uses an inclusive term suggests that he intended to include women among the false teachers.

Notice, too, all the parallels between Paul's descriptions of the false teachers and women in the church in Ephesus. For example, Paul mentions that some false teachers had turned to meaningless talk and later he mentions that some women talked nonsense:

- *Some have departed from these and have turned to meaningless talk.* (1 Timothy 1:6)

- [Younger widows] *become idlers, but also busybodies who talk nonsense, saying things they ought not to.* (1 Timothy 5:13)

Also, some false teachers abandoned the faith and followed demonic teachings, and later Paul mentions some women who broke their first pledge and turned to follow Satan:

- *The Spirit clearly says that in later times, some will abandon the faith and follow deceiving spirits and things taught by demons.* (1 Timothy 4:1)

- *Thus they* [younger widows] *bring judgment on themselves, because they have broken their first pledge.* (1 Timothy 5:12)

- *Some* [younger widows] *have in fact already turned away to follow Satan.* (1 Timothy 5:15)

And if we look ahead, in 2 Timothy, Paul refers to women who are being misled. They are likely some of the women Paul is referring to in 1 Timothy:

> *gullible women, who are loaded down with sins and are swayed by all kinds of evil desires, always learning but never able to come to a knowledge of the truth.* (2 Timothy 3:6–7)

Finally, remember from Acts 19 that Ephesus was the center for worship of the Greek goddess Artemis, the goddess of fertility. The people were lured by promises of fertility, sexuality, and protection during pregnancy and childbirth. The leaders of this cult were predominantly women. As Christianity won converts from followers of Artemis, it makes sense that they would come with the expectation that women could lead.

DON'T FORGET PRISCILLA

Theo, we are about to talk about verses that many people interpret as pro-hibiting women from teaching men. Before we do that, I want you to think about Priscilla. Remember that Paul met Priscilla and her husband, Aquila, in Corinth and they all worked together:

> *After this, Paul left Athens and went to Corinth. There he met a Jew named Aquila, a native of Pontus, who had recently come from Italy with his wife Priscilla, because Claudius had ordered all Jews to leave Rome. Paul went to see them, and because he was a tentmaker as they were, he stayed and worked with them.* (Acts 18:1–3)

Later, when Paul left Corinth, Priscilla and Aquila went with him. Together, they went to Ephesus:

> *Paul stayed on in Corinth for some time. Then he left the brothers and sisters and sailed for Syria, accompanied by Priscilla and Aquila. Before he sailed, he had his hair cut off at Cenchreae because of a vow he had taken. They arrived at Ephesus, where Paul left Priscilla and Aquila. He himself went into the synagogue and reasoned with the Jews.* (Acts 18:18–19)

That's right, Priscilla and Aquila are in Ephesus! And, Theo, while they are in Ephesus, they are teaching people about Jesus!

> *Meanwhile a Jew named Apollos, a native of Alexandria, came to Ephesus. He was a learned man, with a thorough knowledge of the Scriptures. He had been instructed in the way of the Lord, and he spoke with great fervor and taught about Jesus accurately, though he knew only the baptism of John. He began to speak boldly in the synagogue. When Priscilla and Aquila heard him, they invited him to their home and explained to him the way of God more adequately.* (Acts 18:24–26)

Since Priscilla's name is mentioned first here, contrary to normal Greek convention, it is reasonable to infer that she did at least some of this biblical teaching—and probably most of it—to a *man, with a thorough knowledge of the Scriptures.*[69] Some people say she did not "teach" a man but only "explained to him the way of God more accurately" (NASB). But if her explaining something more accurately is not teaching, what is? Others say that she could only do this because her husband was with her, but no Bible passage says a woman can teach only if her husband accompanies her. Still others say that because she was teaching just one man, this is different from what 1 Timothy 2:12 prohibits, but 2:12 also specifies "to teach a man" (singular). Priscilla was probably Timothy's best resource to correct deceived women in Ephesus, so it is doubtful that Paul would give Timothy instructions that would silence his best resource. Keep Priscilla in mind as we dive deeper into 1 Timothy.

1 TIMOTHY 2:8–12: DEALING WITH THE PROBLEM[70]

False teachers had infiltrated the church at Ephesus. How will Timothy deal with those who had been deceived by the false teachers, keeping in mind that the women spreading these false teachings were ignorant, not willfully deceiving others? The first step is to make sure they have the right mindset, are humble, and are focused on God:

> *Therefore I want the men everywhere to pray, lifting up holy hands without anger or disputing.* (1 Timothy 2:8)

> *I also want the women to dress modestly, with decency and propriety, adorning themselves, not with elaborate hairstyles or gold or pearls or expensive clothes, but with good deeds, appropriate for women who profess to worship God.* (1 Timothy 2:9–10)

This translation makes it sound like Paul wants men to pray, but women only have to dress modestly. However, this is not what Paul is saying. Verse 9 starts

---

69. This must not be due to her social status because Acts 18:2 introduces them as "Aquila and Priscilla."
70. For further discussion, see Payne, *Man and Woman, One in Christ*, 311–397.

with the Greek word *hōsautōs*, which means "likewise." In this case, the pre-vious verse discusses the manner in which men pray. So, the word *hōsautōs* at the start of verse 9 indicates that it is similarly discussing the manner in which women pray.[71] Verse 9, therefore, is better translated, "Similarly, I want women to pray with modest dress . . ."

Paul then addresses the fundamental problem of women who are not properly trained. They should learn in quietness and full submission. The word used for "quietness" means a sense of "calm," as in 1 Timothy 2:2, *"peaceful and quiet lives."* The word for "silence" in 1 Corinthians 14:28, 34 is different. Since quietness should be their response to the teaching, it is natural to understand the submission to apply to the teaching as well:

> *A woman should learn in quietness and full submission.*
> (1 Timothy 2:11)

But this translation hides the fact that the verb "learn" here is a command. Paul is commanding Timothy that these women must learn. Paul is not merely giving advice about how women should learn. This is the only command in this chapter.

But you may ask "Why doesn't Paul tell men to do likewise?" Because the con-text indicates that the main problem Paul is addressing concerns women. And there was already a culture of men learning from rabbis, but they didn't have an established convention regarding how women should be taught.

And then we come to arguably the most controversial verse on the topic of women and teaching:

> *I do not permit a woman to teach or to assume authority over a man;*
> *she must be quiet.* (1 Timothy 2:12)

---

71. All sixteen instances of *hōsautōs* in the New Testament show obvious close parallels between the two statements compared, most of them in multiple details. Every other such instance with a transferable preceding verb must transfer that verb to the *hōsautōs* clause. None has anywhere as little parallel with the prior statement as the NIV's translation above indicates.

We will go through this verse carefully. We must consider four key points when reading this sentence.

First, the verb in the phrase "*I do not permit*" is a present active indicative verb in the Greek. This indicates something that is presently ongoing, so is better translated: "I am not permitting." It does not imply a permanent state, or a universal command, like "*I do not permit*" does.

Second, the word itself, "permit," is never used in the original text of the Bible as a universal command but, instead, indicates temporary permission for a specific situation, as in the following verses:

> He ordered the centurion to keep Paul under guard but to give him some freedom and **permit** his friends to take care of his needs. (Acts 24:23)

> For I do not want to see you now and make only a passing visit; I hope to spend some time with you, if the Lord **permits**. (1 Corinthians 16:7)

> Therefore let us move beyond the elementary teachings about Christ and be taken forward to maturity . . . And God **permitting**, we will do so. (Hebrews 6:1–3)

Paul certainly knows how to exercise authority. He knows how to command people to "do this" or "don't do that." Paul would never say, "I am not permitting you to be sexually immoral." He would say, "Do not be sexually immoral!" So the phrase "I am not permitting" is not how Paul gives permanent commands. Paul issues many permanent commands in his letters, and his letters never use the verb "permit" to give a permanent command.[72]

Third, the word translated "*to assume authority*" is *authentein*. Normally, we would begin by observing where this word is used elsewhere in the Bible to help us understand its usage here. However, this word is not used anywhere else in the Bible. It consists of two other words: *autos*, meaning "by oneself, of one's own initiative," as in "autobiography," and *hentēs*, meaning "who finishes,

---

72. See the evidence above that Paul did not write 1 Corinthians 14:34–35.

achieves." The word stresses the activity of the self, as in "accomplish for one's own advantage." It has a common nuance like "autocrat"—acting unilaterally. Related words usually convey a negative nuance. The most common meaning of this word around Paul's time was "to assume authority that one does not rightfully have."

Fourth, the two verbs here, "*to teach*" and "*to assume authority,*" are joined by the coordinating conjunction *oude*. I discussed this word earlier in the section on Galatians. Paul is not talking about two separate issues, "to teach" and "to assume authority," but about their combination: "to assume authority to teach." In other words, Paul is not prohibiting two separate actions—he is prohibiting the *combination* of teaching and assuming authority.

Let's put those four points together. In the currently ongoing crisis of false teaching, Paul is not permitting the women in Ephesus to assume authority to teach if they do not rightfully have that authority. Women like Priscilla, who had recognized authority to teach (Acts 18:26) and whom Paul greets in this same city in 2 Timothy 4:19, would not be assuming authority to teach since they already had that recognized authority. She would have been a key resource to Timothy in teaching women deceived by false teachings. And finally, do not forget that the one and only command in this passage is "let the women learn" (1 Timothy 2:11 KJV).

1 TIMOTHY 2: ANSWER TO THE MOST COMMON OBJECTION

"Why would Paul specifically limit women from assuming authority to teach a man?"

Paul does not state his reason, but this makes sense because in that culture, as a man, Timothy would not have been permitted to access women's private discussions. Timothy had no culturally acceptable way to monitor what women were teaching other women. Prohibiting a woman specifically from assuming authority to teach "a man," however, is what would occur at typical public church meetings attended by men and women. Paul's specification of "a man" made this a limited rule that Timothy could enforce without offending cultural standards of privacy.

1 TIMOTHY 2:13–15: BACK TO THE GARDEN[73]

After telling Timothy that women should not assume authority if they do not rightfully have that authority to teach a man, but rather must learn, Paul goes on to justify his restriction:

> *For Adam was formed first, then Eve. And Adam was not the one deceived; it was the woman who was deceived and became a sinner. But women will be saved through childbearing—if they continue in faith, love and holiness with propriety.* (1 Timothy 2:13–15)

Theo, it's so easy to misunderstand this passage. Many people read this passage and think it is teaching, "Women should not be teachers or leaders because women are more easily deceived than men." Doesn't it sound like that? But no, that is not what Paul is saying at all. He is saying something totally different. We simply need to look at it in light of the Genesis account.

To help you see this passage in a new light, let's review Adam's behavior in the Garden of Eden. The text of Genesis does not mention Adam during the conversation between the serpent and the woman in Genesis 3:1–5. The text does not imply—and certainly does not state—that the serpent's conversation with the woman occurred at the tree of the knowledge of good and evil. It was only at the tree that Genesis 3:6 states that her husband *"was with her."* To be deceived, someone must be caused to believe something that is not true. If Adam heard the serpent's deceptive words and believed them, then he, too, would have been deceived just like Eve was. But maybe Adam was with her only at the tree of the knowledge of good and evil and not earlier during the conversation with the serpent, and so he was not deceived by the serpent. But still, Adam disobeyed God's command! Remember what happened:

---

73. For further discussion, see Payne, *Man and Woman, One in Christ*, 399–444.

She also gave some to her husband, who was with her, and he ate it.
(Genesis 3:6)

She gave him the fruit—he knew which tree it came from—and he ate it. Unless there was some other conversation the text does not mention, his eating the forbidden fruit does not even rise to the level of "deception." It is flat-out disobedience. What Adam did was dumb for someone God had told, "*when you eat from it you will certainly die*" (2:17). Then when God confronted Adam, he passed the buck, blaming both the woman and, implicitly, God: "*The woman you put here with me—she gave me some fruit from the tree, and I ate it*" (3:12).

Either Adam heard (or overheard) Eve's conversation with the serpent and, therefore, was deceived just like Eve was, or Adam did not hear the conversation, in which case he was clearly disobedient. Nothing that Adam does here is honorable in any way. Nothing worthy of leadership. Nothing worth imitating. Certainly, nothing Paul would look to and say, "Sorry, women, we need more leaders like Adam!"

When Paul says, "*Adam was not the one deceived*," Paul does not mean that Adam passed the test. Adam most definitely did NOT pass the test. Paul is simply highlighting the fact that Adam was not the target of Satan's deception—the serpent did not speak to Adam. The passive voice of the verb in "the woman was deceived (*exapatētheisa*)" implies that the serpent deceived her. It makes it clear that the serpent, Satan, targeted the woman and deceived her into disobeying God's command.

Theo, can you think of any more powerful example of the danger of women being deceived by Satan than this? Consider the immediate context in Ephesus. Women were leading without proper training. Sin was continuing to enter the church through the women, just as it had in the Garden of Eden. Women continued to be victims of deception and Paul's solution is clear. He wants the women to learn, and to learn well. Then they can become solid leaders not prone to deception.

There have been numerous attempts to explain the meaning of *"shall be saved through childbearing"* (2:15). The Greek word here is a noun, "childbirth," not a verb. In surviving Greek literature prior to Paul, the word "childbirth" always refers to the birth of a child, not the process of childbearing. Additionally, there is an article, "the," in front of the word "childbirth." So, Paul says women will be saved specifically through "the childbirth."[74] Which childbirth is Paul referring to? Presumably, the only child ever born who can save anybody— Jesus! Indeed, Paul had just written *"Christ Jesus came into the world to save sinners"* (1:15), and shortly thereafter wrote, *"He appeared in the flesh"* (3:16). Furthermore, almost immediately after Genesis 3:13's "The serpent deceived me" that Paul cites in 1 Timothy 2:14 is God's promise that "the seed of the woman" *"will crush your head, and you will strike his heel"* (Genesis 3:15). This is known as the *protoevangelium*, the first announcement of salvation by the suffering of the seed of the woman who would overcome Satan. Timothy, who was well trained in Scripture and by Paul, who refers to Christ as "the seed" in Galatians 3:19,[75] would understand this reference.

Every other instance of any word related to "save" (*sōzō*) in Paul's letters conveys spiritual salvation. Furthermore, this fits the conditions that follow perfectly: *"if they continue in faith, love, and holiness."* This is an encouraging and empowering message for women. Our Savior is the promised "seed of the woman" who on the cross saved us from the sin that resulted from Satan's deception. This sentence does not teach that "women should stay home and make babies." It is best translated "anyone will be saved through the Childbirth [Jesus] if they . . ."[76]

---

74. Of the 61 instances of an article ("the") in 1–2 Timothy and Titus, only one clearly refers to something in general, such as "childbearing." Of the rest, 55 are clearly individualizing, so it is most natural to understand this as a reference to one particular childbirth.

75. Cf. Paul's other references to Christ as the "seed" in Romans 1:3; Galatians 3:16; 2 Timothy 2:8.

76. Neither "will be saved" nor "if they continue" is feminine, nor does either have with it a feminine pronoun as subject. Everything in this sentence applies equally well to all believers. The subject "anyone" best explains the shift from singular ("anyone will be saved") to plural ("if they continue"). Dorothy A. Lee, *The Ministry of Women in the New Testament: Reclaiming the Biblical Vision for Church Leadership* (Grand Rapids, MI: Baker, 2021) 128 also argues for the translation: "will be saved through the Childbirth, if they . . ."

1 Timothy 3:1–7: Overseer Qualifications[77]

In 1 Timothy 3, we find a list of qualifications for the positions of overseer and deacon. First, he gives the overseer qualifications:

> *Here is a trustworthy saying: Whoever aspires to be an overseer desires a noble task. Now the overseer is to be above reproach, faithful to his wife, temperate, self-controlled, respectable, hospitable, able to teach, not given to drunkenness, not violent but gentle, not quarrelsome, not a lover of money. He must manage his own family well and see that his children obey him, and he must do so in a manner worthy of full respect. (If anyone does not know how to manage his own family, how can he take care of God's church?) He must not be a recent convert, or he may become conceited and fall under the same judgment as the devil. He must also have a good reputation with outsiders, so that he will not fall into disgrace and into the devil's trap. (1 Timothy 3:1–7)*

When Paul writes "whoever" (literally, "if anyone"), he uses the Greek word *tis,* which, as I mentioned before, is an inclusive, completely gender-neutral term. It could be misleading to use *tis* to describe a group limited to males. Remember also that Paul just got through talking about men and women. He had men and women on the brain. If he had any intention to teach that only men should be overseers, he would have said something like "Any man who aspires the office of overseer desires a noble task." But Paul does not say "man" or "he." Paul says "whoever" because Paul means "whoever"—man or woman.

Second, although the CEV and CEB accurately reflect the Greek by having no "he," "him," or "his" in 1 Timothy 3:1–7 or Titus 1:5–9, most translations add many masculine pronouns like "he," "him," and "his" to these paragraphs. The ESV adds fourteen, and the NIV adds seventeen! Paul, however, does not include a single "he," "him," or "his" in the overseer qualifications here or in the elder qualifications in Titus 1:5–9. Those translators probably added

---

77. For further discussion, see Payne, *Man and Woman, One in Christ*, 445–454.

masculine pronouns to make it sound better in English and because they assumed that only males could be overseers.

What is left then to restrict women from being an overseer? Well, the word for "*the overseer*" in 3:2 is a masculine noun, but the word for "the office of overseer" in 3:1 is a feminine noun. Neither implies that overseers must be women or men. It was simply Greek convention when groups of people are addressed to use the masculine form of a noun.[78] Timothy Friberg counted between 7,500 and 8,000 instances in the New Testament, almost one per sentence, where a masculine form either must or could apply to women.[79] Accordingly, merely the presence of one or more masculine nouns or adjectives should not be used to exclude women from this text or any other passage about a group of people.

This leaves us with only one expression in this paragraph that has been used to exclude women. Paul says that an overseer must be a *mias gunaikos andra*, a "man of one woman." It is typically translated "*faithful to his wife.*" The closest English equivalent word is "monogamous," which can refer to either men or women. While the word here for "man" can also just mean "person," here it is combined with "of one woman," so it naturally means "man." That by itself, however, does not limit overseers to men.

Note that none of the three words by themselves means "*faithful.*" It is the combination of the three words together that forms an idiom—a figure of speech—meaning "*faithful person.*" This idiom acts like a noun, and like many Greek nouns, it comes in masculine and feminine forms. By Greek convention, when both men and women are being described, the masculine form is the one that is used, as here.

---

78. James Hope Moulton, *An Introduction to the Study of New Testament Greek* (5th ed. revised by Rev. Henry G. Meecham; London: Epworth Press, 1955) 109. Also, Gordon Hugenberger states "In the absence of other constraints, norms that utilize male-oriented terminology ought to be construed in general as including both sexes in their purview." G. H. Hugenberger, "Women in Church Office: Hermeneutics or Exegesis? A Survey of Approaches to 1 Timothy 2:8–15," *JETS* 35/3 (1992) 341–360, at 360 note 78.
79. Personal correspondence.

But Paul uses the feminine form later in chapter 5 when he is describing which widows should be put on the list of people to receive assistance. One requirement Paul lists is that the widow needs to have been *"faithful to her husband."* The phrase Paul uses in 1 Timothy 5:9 for marital faithfulness is *henos andros gynē,* or literally, "woman of one man." Paul uses the feminine form of the idiom there because "widows" are exclusively female.

So, when Paul tells Timothy that overseers should be faithful people, he can only use the masculine or the feminine form of the idiom. There is no gender-neutral form of the idiom. I'm not even sure what a gender-neutral version of this idiom might be—"one spouse spouse?" It was conventional, however, when referring to a group of people who might be either men or women to use the masculine form of the idiom—the feminine form is only used when the group is exclusively female. Therefore, although the idiomatic phrase "man of one woman" *includes* men as potential overseers, it does not *exclude* women.

The eloquent Greek church father, John Chrysostom, who knew Hellenistic Greek better than anyone alive today, confirms this. He writes regarding "men of one woman" in 1 Timothy 3:12: "Deacons must be men of one woman. This is appropriate to say regarding women deacons also."[80] Other prominent theologians like Thomas Schreiner also acknowledge that "man of one woman" does not exclude women from the office of overseer.[81]

In summary, Paul starts out this paragraph with his thesis statement that *anybody* who wants to become an overseer desires a good thing. This encourages women to desire becoming an overseer, and nothing else in this paragraph overrules that. None of the qualifications exclude women.

---

80. John Chrysostom (AD 347–407), Bishop of Constantinople, *Homily 11 on 1 Timothy 3.* He acknowledged this even though he opposed women being in leadership!

81. Thomas R. Schreiner, "Philip Payne on Familiar Ground: A Review of Philip B. Payne, Man and Woman, One in Christ: An Exegetical and Theological Study of Paul's Letters," *Journal of Biblical Manhood and Womanhood* (Spring 2010) 33–46, at 35, acknowledges, "The requirements for elders in 1 Tim 3:1–7 and Titus 1:6–9, including the statement that they are to be one-woman men, does not necessarily in and of itself preclude women from serving as elders."

1 Timothy 3:8–13: Deacon Qualifications[82]

Paul follows up his list of overseer qualifications with a list of qualifications for deacons:

> *In the same way, deacons are to be worthy of respect, sincere, not indulging in much wine, and not pursuing dishonest gain. They must keep hold of the deep truths of the faith with a clear conscience. They must first be tested; and then if there is nothing against them, let them serve as deacons. In the same way, the women are to be worthy of respect, not malicious talkers but temperate and trustworthy in everything. A deacon must be faithful to his wife and must manage his children and his household well. Those who have served well gain an excellent standing and great assurance in their faith in Christ Jesus.* (1 Timothy 3:8–13)

Paul begins both verse 8 and verse 11 with "*In the same way* (hōsautōs) . . ." to cause readers to add the implied verb from verse 2, "It is necessary for [deacons] to be . . ." Verse 8 identifies four requirements: "*deacons are to be worthy of respect, sincere, not indulging in much wine, and not pursuing dishonest gain.*"

In verse 11, Paul repeats essentially these same four qualifications in the same order for women deacons: "*In the same way,* [women deacons] *are to be worthy of respect, not malicious talkers, but temperate, and trustworthy in everything.*" Paul's "in the same way" (hōsautōs) and the repetition of nearly identical qualifications listed in the same order demonstrate that in both verses, he is listing requirements for a church office. Since Paul has just specified that he is listing qualifications for the office of deacon and since the next verse continues with other qualifications for deacons, we know that these are requirements for women deacons.

---

82. For further discussion, see Payne, *Man and Woman, One in Christ*, 454–459.

The word used for "women" in verse 11 can refer to either women or wives, depending on the context. When it refers to wives, this is typically accompanied by a prior reference to husbands followed by "their wives," or if the context is about wives, "the wives." Regarding deacons, however, no reference is made to husbands, and the context is not about marriage. Verse 11 makes no mention of "their" wives, nor does it even have an article that might imply "the wives." Furthermore, it makes sense for Paul to list the qualifications for women deacons, but it does not make sense to list qualifications for the wives of deacons if they do not hold a church office. Besides, Paul does not list qualifications for the wives of the higher office, overseers (or the husbands of overseers, for that matter), so interpreting "women" as meaning "wives of deacons" simply does not fit the context.

In verse 12, Paul continues the qualifications for deacons, saying, "*A deacon must be faithful to his wife.*" As you might expect, the phrase referring to marital faithfulness is the plural form of the same idiom as before, "men of one woman." And as discussed in the previous section on "Overseer Qualifications," the idiom follows the common convention of using male-oriented terminology to refer to both men and women and therefore cannot be used to exclude women. The specific reference to women deacons in verse 11 makes it clear that "men of one woman" in verse 12 does not exclude women deacons. John Chrysostom's *Homily 11 on 1 Timothy 3* confirms this: "Men of one woman . . . is appropriate to say regarding women deacons also."

Titus: Welcome to Crete

Paul and Titus worked together in Crete planting churches (Titus 1:5). Titus was a wonderful, encouraging brother in Christ. He is mentioned many times in 2 Corinthians, like:

> *But God, who comforts the downcast, comforted us by the coming of Titus . . .* (2 Corinthians 7:6)

> *Thanks be to God, who put into the heart of Titus the same concern I have for you. For Titus not only welcomed our appeal, but he is coming to you with much enthusiasm and on his own initiative.* (2 Corinthians 8:16–17)

Theo, you should understand the rebellious people Titus faced in Crete. Just look at how Paul talks about the Cretans:

> *For there are many rebellious people, full of meaningless talk and deception, especially those of the circumcision group. They must be silenced, because they are disrupting whole households by teaching things they ought not to teach—and that for the sake of dishonest gain. One of Crete's own prophets has said it: "Cretans are always liars, evil brutes, lazy gluttons." This saying is true. Therefore rebuke them sharply, so that they will be sound in the faith and will pay no attention to Jewish myths or to the merely human commands of those who reject the truth. To the pure, all things are pure, but to those who are corrupted and do not believe, nothing is pure. In fact, both their minds and consciences are corrupted. They claim to know God, but by their actions they deny him. They are detestable, disobedient and unfit for doing anything good.* (Titus 1:10–16)

Paul eventually left Crete, and it was Titus's job to continue the work there.

TITUS 1:6–9: ELDER QUALIFICATIONS[83]

The first and main task for Titus was to appoint elders who would be able to lead the churches in Crete to address the numerous challenges they faced. Paul lists these qualifications for the elders:

> *The reason I left you in Crete was that you might put in order what was left unfinished and appoint elders in every town, as I directed you. An elder must be blameless, faithful to his wife, a man whose children believe and are not open to the charge of being wild and disobedient. Since an overseer manages God's household, he must be blameless— not overbearing, not quick-tempered, not given to drunkenness, not violent, not pursuing dishonest gain. Rather, he must be hospitable, one who loves what is good, who is self-controlled, upright, holy and disciplined. He must hold firmly to the trustworthy message as it has been taught, so that he can encourage others by sound doctrine and refute those who oppose it.* (Titus 1:5–9)*

This passage is very similar to 1 Timothy 3, so I will refer you to that section if you have not already read it. Here again, Paul uses the Greek word *tis* ("whoever," which includes both men and women) in 1:6 to describe the potential elder. The word "man" that the NIV adds is not in the Greek text. Paul again requires marital faithfulness using the phrase "man of one woman," which cannot be used to exclude women. And once again, there are no words such as "he," "him," or "his" in the Greek text. So, as before, all the qualifications for elder are just as appropriate for women as for men.

---

83. For further discussion, see Payne, *Man and Woman, One in Christ*, 445–449, 459.

TITUS 2:1–10: INSTRUCTIONS FOR ELDERS[84]

You, however, must teach what is appropriate to sound doctrine. Teach the older men to be temperate, worthy of respect, self-controlled, and sound in faith, in love and in endurance. Likewise, teach the older women to be reverent in the way they live, not to be slanderers or addicted to much wine, but to teach what is good. Then they can urge the younger women to love their husbands and children, to be self-controlled and pure, to be busy at home, to be kind, and to be subject to their husbands, so that no one will malign the word of God. Similarly, encourage the young men to be self-controlled. In everything set them an example by doing what is good. In your teaching show integrity, seriousness and soundness of speech that cannot be condemned, so that those who oppose you may be ashamed because they have nothing bad to say about us. (Titus 2:1–8)

Okay, Theo, I have another pop quiz for you:

Q: What is an "elder"?

    a.   A church officer or

    b.   An old person?

Let's see if we can figure it out. When Paul mentions elders in the previous chapter (Titus 1:5), he is referring to the church office of elder and he uses the Greek word *presbyteros*.[85] But the word translated "older man" in Titus 2:2 is a slightly different word, *presbytēs*.[86] You might be tempted, therefore, to think that there is a simple rule:

$$presbyteros = \text{"church elder"}$$

$$presbytēs = \text{"old man"}$$

---

84. For further discussion, see Payne, *Man and Woman, One in Christ*, 330, 352, 392.
85. Paul also uses the word, *presbyterous*, which is the accusative form of the word *presbyteros*.
86. Paul also uses the word, *presbytas*, which is the accusative form of the word *presbytēs*.

Unfortunately, although that would be a nice, simple rule, it is wrong. For example, in 1 Timothy 5:1, Paul tells Timothy not to rebuke older men, using the same word that in Titus 1:5 means church "elder," *presbyteros*. So, the rule now looks like this:

presbyteros = "church elder" or "old man"

presbytēs = "old man"

But *presbytēs* can also refer to the office of "elder." For example, Lamentations 4:16 says, "*The priests are shown no honor, the elders* (presbytas) *no favor*" and Numbers 10:31 (Greek text) says, "You will be an elder (*presbytēs*) among us." So, our rule now looks like this:

presbyteros = "church elder" or "old man"

presbytēs = "church elder" or "old man"

Either term can refer to a church "elder." Since both *presbyteros* and *presbytēs* can mean either "church elder" or "old man," we must examine how they are used in each context to determine their meaning. The key question is whether what Paul says in Titus 2:1–8 is more appropriate regarding old people or regarding church elders. Some commentaries argue as follows:

> Although the word Paul uses for "old women" is the exact word that would mean "female elders,"[87] Paul cannot possibly be referring to female elders because there is no such thing as a female elder.

Theo, I hope that the gaping flaw in that logic is clear to you. If you assume that women cannot be elders, this will force you to the conclusion that Paul is referring to old women (and therefore, that this entire passage is simply about old or young men or women). Instead, we should come to this passage with no such preconception. If we do that, the close association of the content of these

---

87. *Presbytidas* in Titus 2:3 is precisely the same form of the same word that the Council of Laodicea canon XI used to forbid the appointment of "female elders."

verses with Paul's passages about elders will lead us to the conclusion that Paul is referring to the office of elders here.

In Titus 2:2, he gives instructions to elders in general, then specific instructions for female elders, and then instructions regarding young elders, like Titus, whom Paul addresses as *"my true son"* in 1:4. Seven reasons cause me to believe that these groups of people Paul is talking about are church elders, not simply old or young men or women.

First, it would be completely natural at this point in the letter for Paul to give instructions for the elders Titus had appointed. Immediately after the introductory greeting in chapter 1, Paul reminds Titus of his mission in Crete to appoint elders. After listing the qualifications of elders, Paul describes the urgency of appointing elders in Crete. Here, at the start of chapter 2, it makes sense that Paul would now instruct Titus regarding what he should be teaching these recently appointed elders. Later, in chapter 3, Paul will eventually get around to giving Titus some commands for all the people in the churches in Crete. But here at the start of chapter 2, Paul is still focused on elders.

Second, this passage starts with Paul telling Titus to *"teach what is appropriate to sound doctrine."* This parallels Paul's earlier stated desire for elders to *"encourage others by sound doctrine and refute those who oppose it"* (1:9, also 1 Timothy 3:2). This focus on teaching sound doctrine is more appropriate for elders than for groups distinguished only by age and sex.

Third, if Paul had intended Titus to convey four messages to four groups of old and young distinguished by sex, one would expect a straightforward listing of the four groups, like what Paul does in 1 Timothy 5:1–2:

> *Do not rebuke an older man harshly, but exhort him as if he were your father. Treat younger men as brothers, older women as mothers, and younger women as sisters, with absolute purity.*

Titus 2:2–8, however, gives instructions for three groups, each set of instructions connected by "similarly" (*hōsautōs*, which I discussed in earlier sections).

Fourth, all the commands in Titus 2:2–8 closely parallel the qualifications Paul gave for elders in Titus 1:5–9 and 1 Timothy 3:1–7[88] and/or deacons in 1 Timothy 3:8–13:

- He tells the elders in Titus 2:2 to be:

    - *temperate—Nēphalios* is a requirement for overseers (1 Timothy 3:2) and women deacons (1 Timothy 3:11).

    - *worthy of respect—Semnos* is the first requirement for both deacons and women deacons (1 Timothy 3:8, 11).

    - *self-controlled— Sōphrōn* is a requirement for both elders (Titus 1:8) and overseers (1 Timothy 3:2).

    - *sound in faith—*repeats the word for "sound," *hugiainō,* used in the parallel "faith" requirement for elders in Titus 1:9: *"hold firmly to the trustworthy message as it has been taught"* and parallels the "faith" requirement for deacons in 1 Timothy 3:9.

    - *[sound in] love—*This is similar to the requirements for elder, *"lover of goodness"* (Titus 1:8), and overseer (1 Timothy 3:2), *"hospitable."*

    - *[sound in] endurance—*This is similar both to the *"not . . . a recent convert"* overseer requirement (1 Timothy 3:6) and the "faithful in all things" (NASB) female deacon requirement (1 Timothy 3:11).

- Similarly, all of Paul's instructions for female elders in Titus 2:3 parallel the requirements for elders and/or deacons:

    - *not . . . slanderers—Mē diabolous,* a word used twice regarding overseers (1 Timothy 3:6–7), here identical to the requirement for female deacons (1 Timothy 3:11)

    - [not] *addicted to much wine* (Titus 1:7; 1 Timothy 3:2, 3, 8 with identical *mē oinō pollō,* 11)

    - *teach what is good* (Titus 1:9; 1 Timothy 3:2).

---

88. Note that elders = overseers in Titus 1:5, 7; Acts 20:17, 28; 1 Peter 5:1–2.

- Finally, he commands Titus to encourage the young elders like himself to be *"self-controlled"—Sōphrōn*, required of both elders (Titus 1:8) and overseers (1 Timothy 3:2).

All these instructions are especially important for elders, and many of them do not describe people in general. For example, it would be unrealistic to command all older men, especially new believers, to be *"sound in faith . . . and in endurance,"* or all older women to be teachers of *"what is good"* because these take time and training.

Fifth, the word the NIV translates "reverent" (*hieroprepēs*) in Titus 2:3 means "like those employed in sacred service" or suitable for "a sacred place, person, or matter." It combines *hieros*, "pertinent to being of transcendent purity, holy" or "filled with or manifesting divine power," and *prepō*, "be fitting." Whenever the related word *hieron* occurs in the New Testament, it refers to the temple in Jerusalem (e.g., 1 Corinthians 9:13). Urging behavior "befitting the temple" is more appropriate for female elders than old women.

Sixth, Paul commands Titus in 2:3 to teach the second group to be "teachers of what is excellent (*kalodidaskalous*)," a word Paul apparently coined himself. Since teaching is a task assigned to elders (Titus 1:8; 1 Timothy 3:2), it is most appropriate to understand this group as female elders.

Seventh, Paul continues this same sentence (Titus 2:6–8) by commanding Titus to be a model to other young elders of "good deeds (*kalōn ergōn*), in teaching with integrity, seriousness, and sound speech that cannot be condemned." The RSV and NRSV separate "in your teaching" from "good deeds" by adding "and," but there is no conjunction in Greek. The NIV even puts "in your teaching" into a totally separate sentence! But these are all incorrect translations.

Paul is not telling Titus to simply "do good deeds." In Greek, "in teaching" follows in the same sentence immediately after "model of good deeds" and so highlights the particular "good deeds" Paul wants Titus to model. Therefore, Paul is calling Titus to be an example to them "in teaching with integrity." But why does Titus need to set an example of good teaching? Because Paul wants these young elders to follow Titus's model by teaching with integrity. Teaching is a task assigned to elders, so this command fits church elders best.

What Paul writes regarding all three groups, therefore, is more appropriate for elders than different groups distinguished only by age and sex. Everything Paul writes about all three groups is appropriate for church elders. The first group could be understood as referring specifically to male elders, or it could refer generically to all elders since the masculine form is the normal form used in Greek for generic reference without restriction to men.

TITUS 2: ANSWERS TO COMMON OBJECTIONS

"The older women (elders) are told to teach only younger women."

Paul did not write that these women may teach *only* younger women. The text gives examples of what female elders teach as "teachers of what is excellent," but it does not restrict their teaching either in scope or audience. Paul's praise for Timothy's grandmother, Lois, and mother, Eunice, for teaching him the Holy Scriptures (2 Timothy 1:5; 3:14–15) shows that younger women were not the only group older women could and should teach and that the scope of their teaching includes the Holy Scriptures.

"But church elders cannot be young! Therefore, the people that Paul is talking about are not church elders."

A church "elder" was someone selected for spiritual maturity. Paul commissioned Titus to "*appoint elders* (plural) *in every town*" (Titus 1:5) and every qualification regards spiritual maturity. Paul gave no age requirement. It is clear from the responsibilities Paul assigned to Titus in Crete, including teaching (Titus 1:9; 2:1, 7), and to Timothy in Ephesus that they were both overseers. Both were young. We know this because Paul calls Titus "*my true son*" (1:4), and he tells Timothy "*Don't let anyone look down on you because you are young*" (1 Timothy 4:12). It is doubtful that all the small house churches Titus was overseeing in Crete would have multiple mature believers of an "old" age. Since Titus was not an "elder" in years but had the oversight function of an elder, it is only natural that some of the elders he appointed for these small churches would also be young.

TITUS 2:4–5: SUBJECTION OF YOUNGER WOMEN[89]

I want to discuss part of the previous passage separately. Here, Paul commands Titus to teach these women elders to instruct the younger women as follows:

> *Then they can urge the younger women to love their husbands and children, to be self-controlled and pure, to be busy at home, to be kind, and to be subject to their husbands, so that no one will malign the word of God.* (Titus 2:4–5)

"*Urge the younger women to love their husbands*" shows that just as husbands should love their wives, wives should also love their husbands. This proves that it is false to think that Paul's commands "to submit" and "to love" in Ephesians 5 apply, respectively, only to wives and only to husbands. Paul's command for wives to submit is one expression of "submitting to one another." So it must also apply to husbands.

Most of these qualities are reminiscent of the noble wife in Proverbs 31:10–31, and all of them describe "good wives" in Paul's day. Note that Paul is talking specifically about younger women here who are urged to "*love their husbands,*" "*be busy at home,*" and "*be subject to their husbands.*" Not all women have husbands, so the husband-related instructions here should not be interpreted as commands for all women.

Paul gives a specific reason for telling younger women to be subject to their husbands, and it is not because that is how God designed marriage. It was, "*so that no one will malign the word of God.*" That's right. Paul wants younger

---

89. For further discussion, see Payne, *Man and Woman, One in Christ*, 330, 352, 392.

women to be subject to their husbands so that they adhere to cultural norms, and as a result, others will speak well of the gospel. Greek literature confirms that wives in that culture were expected to do each of the things Paul lists here. Because wives who weren't submissive undermined conventional norms, they could lead people to reject the gospel. Similarly, just a few verses later, Titus 2:9–10 calls *"slaves to be subject to their masters in everything . . . so that in every way they will make the teaching about God our Savior attractive."* By being submissive, according to cultural norms, both wives and slaves made the gospel more attractive, especially to their husbands and masters. We will see this idea repeated in the next section about 1 Peter.

1 Peter 3:1–7: Husband-Wife Mutual Submission and the Wife as Weaker[90]

In 1 Peter 3, Peter commands wives to submit themselves to their husbands and describes wives as the "weaker partner" in a marriage. Before we get to those verses, we should discuss the context of the first two chapters.

Remember, Theo, back in Acts, Luke explains that after the stoning of Stephen, Christians were persecuted and scattered among the nations.

> *And Saul approved of their killing* [Stephen]. *On that day a great persecution broke out against the church in Jerusalem, and all except the apostles were scattered throughout Judea and Samaria. Godly men buried Stephen and mourned deeply for him. But Saul began to destroy the church. Going from house to house, he dragged off both men and women and put them in prison.* (Acts 8:1–3)

In this letter, Peter is now writing to those exiles who are living among non-Christians, and subject to non-Christian authorities, to encourage them during their time of suffering. Peter knows that life is difficult for Christian exiles. But most of them have no viable alternative, so they are stuck in their present situation, however dangerous or painful it may be.

> *Peter, an apostle of Jesus Christ, To God's elect, exiles scattered throughout the provinces of Pontus, Galatia, Cappadocia, Asia and Bithynia . . . In all this you greatly rejoice, though now for a little while you may have had to suffer grief in all kinds of trials.* (1 Peter 1:1, 6)

> *Dear friends, do not be surprised at the fiery ordeal that has come on you to test you, as though something strange were happening to you. But rejoice inasmuch as you participate in the sufferings of Christ, so that you may be overjoyed when his glory is revealed. If you are insulted*

---

90. For further discussion, see Payne, *Man and Woman, One in Christ*, 276.

*because of the name of Christ, you are blessed, for the Spirit of glory
and of God rests on you. If you suffer, it should not be as a murderer or
thief or any other kind of criminal, or even as a meddler. However, if
you suffer as a Christian, do not be ashamed, but praise God that you
bear that name. For it is time for judgment to begin with God's household; and if it begins with us, what will the outcome be for those who
do not obey the gospel of God? And, "If it is hard for the righteous to be
saved, what will become of the ungodly and the sinner?" So then, those
who suffer according to God's will should commit themselves to their
faithful Creator and continue to do good.* (1 Peter 4:12–19)

The best Peter can do is to encourage them to stay strong in the faith and to
give them hope that if they lead exemplary lives, they may be able to win over
unbelievers. And, while doing that, Peter tells them to submit to whatever
authority they find themselves under:

*Dear friends, I urge you, as foreigners and exiles, to abstain from sin-
ful desires, which wage war against your soul. Live such good lives
among the pagans that, though they accuse you of doing wrong, they
may see your good deeds and glorify God on the day he visits us. Submit yourselves for the Lord's sake to every human authority: whether
to the emperor, as the supreme authority, or to governors, who are sent
by him to punish those who do wrong and to commend those who do
right. For it is God's will that by doing good you should silence the
ignorant talk of foolish people. Live as free people, but do not use your
freedom as a cover-up for evil; live as God's slaves. Show proper respect
to everyone, love the family of believers, fear God, honor the emperor.*
(1 Peter 2:11–17)

He then specifically offers hope to slaves, wives, and husbands. But, Theo,
remember that these are Christian slaves, wives, and husbands who are living
"among the pagans." He is not describing warm Christian fellowship. He is
rather trying to give hope and guidance to the body of Christ, so they can get
through this time of trial.

First, he calls the Christian exiles who are slaves to submit to their masters, even harsh, abusive masters. Clearly, in this passage, Peter is trying to make the best of a horrible situation and is not advocating slavery itself. Then, likewise, he calls the exiled Christian women to submit to their husbands:

> *Wives, in the same way submit yourselves to your own husbands so that, if any of them do not believe the word, they may be won over without words by the behavior of their wives, when they see the purity and reverence of your lives. Your beauty should not come from outward adornment, such as elaborate hairstyles and the wearing of gold jewelry or fine clothes. Rather, it should be that of your inner self, the unfading beauty of a gentle and quiet spirit, which is of great worth in God's sight. For this is the way the holy women of the past who put their hope in God used to adorn themselves. They submitted themselves to their own husbands, like Sarah, who obeyed Abraham and called him her lord. You are her daughters if you do what is right and do not give way to fear.* (1 Peter 3:1–6)

Repeating his hope and plan, Peter wants wives to submit to their husbands to win them over to Christ. Even in their weaker social standing, Peter calls them courageously to identify with their Lord Jesus Christ, in spite of the social expectation that wives adopt the religious beliefs of their husbands.

Finally, Peter commands husbands to submit themselves to their wives.

> *Husbands, in the same way be considerate as you live with your wives, and treat them with respect as the weaker partner and as heirs with you of the gracious gift of life, so that nothing will hinder your prayers.* (1 Peter 3:7)

Theo, you probably noticed that the word "submit" is not in the NIV translation of this verse. The NIV here says "be considerate," but that verb is not present in the original text. In Greek, this sentence has no main verb. The phrase "in the same way" means we need to look to previous verses to figure out which verb to use here, and each of the three preceding sections begins with a command to "submit":

- 2:13 *Submit yourselves for the Lord's sake to every human authority*

- 2:18 *Slaves, in reverent fear of God submit yourselves to your masters*

- 3:1 *Wives, in the same way* (homoiōs) *submit yourselves to your own husbands*

So, when Peter writes in 1 Peter 3:7, "*Husbands, in the same way* (homoiōs)," the only command supplied by the context is "submit." The parallel with 3:1 implies "*Husbands, in the same way* submit to your own wives." This permits the rest of the sentence to flow naturally: "dwelling together wisely, recognizing her as a feminine[91] precious vessel, and lavish them with honor as co-heirs with you of the gracious gift of life, so that your prayers won't be hindered."

Peter's description of the wives as "*heirs with you of the gracious gift of life*" shows the wives' equal standing in Christ with their husbands. This contrasts sharply with women's unequal and disadvantaged legal position regarding such things as inheritance in Peter's day. "*Treat them with respect*" uses the Greek noun for "honor." This conveys social status to the believing wife that is exceptional in that culture.

There is one last phrase to look at, where Peter describes wives as the "*weaker partner.*" Peter does not tell us what he means by this. The phrase "weaker partner" may mean that wives tend to be physically weaker than husbands, so the husbands should treat their wives with consideration and respect and not use their strength to their advantage. "Weaker" may also refer to the wife's weaker social position in that culture. The Greek phrase is "weaker vessel." The use of "vessel" for a pottery container with the adjective "weaker" in the context of "joint heirs" suggests a fragile, precious vessel. Although women were regarded as weaker than men in that culture, they are precious in God's sight. Indeed, they are full inheritors in Christ.

---

91. BDAG 208, *gynaikeios* "feminine."

"*So that nothing will hinder your* [plural] *prayers*" implies serious conse-quences for husbands who do not submit to and honor their wives. It gives God pleasure for husbands to relinquish their socially sanctioned power over their wives and to honor them as the equals they are in God's sight.

In summary, Theo, Peter was writing to give guidance to Christians living as exiles in a pagan land. It is striking that just as Paul commands wives and hus-bands to submit to one another in Ephesians 5:21–22, Peter also commands wives and husbands to submit to one another and for husbands to honor their wives as joint heirs of the gracious gift of life (3:7).

Conclusions

NOT SO SIMPLE, BUT WORTH IT

Dear Theo,

I think that covers just about every passage that talks about male-female equality. I came to the Bible desiring to listen to what the Spirit says about men and women and to do my best to understand God's Word as originally written. I trust that you have been listening to what the Bible says about God desiring men and women to serve and lead alongside each other within the church and family, as equals, in whatever ways they are gifted.

But I do not want you to think that my simplification of this topic means that the theology is simple or that every nuance has been definitively resolved. I acknowledge the many theologians, historians, and others who have wrestled with these passages. Behind every verse we have considered, there are nuances that they are continuing to wrestle with even today. If you want to dig deeper, I encourage you to visit the website of CBE International (**www.cbe-international.org**), where you will find a treasure trove of related resources and discussions.

I also do not want you to think that the task ahead (men and women working together as equals) is simple. I have heard many people say something like, "If we don't let the men be in charge, they won't participate in anything." I have heard of some churches where this seems to be the case; there are many women in leadership, but no men. I am sure there are many reasons for this, including men not wanting (or knowing how) to work with women, or women not wanting (or knowing how) to work with men. But this is obviously not how churches or families should operate. We do not want to swap out exclusively male leadership for exclusively female leadership. There is too much work to do for either half of God's people to sit on the sidelines.

It will take continued work to navigate this new reality. Years ago, Billy Graham had rules where he would never have one-on-one private meetings with a woman, to keep from having any appearance of impropriety. This rule did solidify his reputation, and other Christian leaders might have been saved from grave sins and humiliation if they had followed similar rules. Christians in particularly prominent positions have always been targeted by Satan, fairly or unfairly, and all of us fallen creatures are vulnerable to temptation. However, making this a rigid rule excludes women from important discussions. Women are disenfranchised if they can only have one-on-one meetings with other women. Jesus's own life is our model and can help us figure out how best to work with each other now. As Leanne Weber writes:

> We need to see our colleagues, regardless of gender, as equal co-workers and partners in the kingdom of God rather than as "distractions." We must dare to follow Jesus's example from Scripture when he spent time alone with the Samaritan woman (which was two strikes against him!) without any thought of what others may think of him. Worrying about what others think is not the best way to set workplace or church policies … It is important that we begin building an atmosphere of trust and cooperation between male and female colleagues in our society, but especially in the church. God has created us as equals and given us gifts according to what he wants us to accomplish. Common sense, respect, and personal integrity should win over suspicion and distrust every time.[92]

It may not be easy to know what to do. And it may not be easy to do it. But the goal of equality is absolutely worth it!

And with that, it's time to close out this letter. So many people have spoken eloquently on this topic, but I will let Graham Joseph Hill have the last word:

---

92. Weber, "Moving Beyond the Billy Graham Rule," Jan 29, 2020, https://www. cbeinternational.org/resource/article/mutuality-blog-magazine/moving-beyond-billy-graham-rule

We need to guide men and women toward honoring, respecting, and relating to each other as equal partners and coheirs with Christ, and the church can do this well by helping both men and women become disciples who imitate Christ Jesus . . . Healthy personal identity grows when we focus on discipleship and conformity to Christ. And when we focus on this kind of discipleship, we also foster healthy relationships between the sexes.[93]

I cannot say it any better than that.

Theo, thank you again for giving me an excuse to write this letter! I look forward to hearing your thoughts, and I am happy to talk with you more about it at any time.

Grace and I eagerly look forward to seeing you and Ruth again soon!

Love,
Uncle Johnny

93. Hill, "Let's Stop Talking about Masculinity and Start Talking about Discipleship," Jan 8, 2020, https://www.cbeinternational.org/resource/article/mutuality-blog-magazine/lets-stop-talking-about-masculinity-and-start-talking